Voyager Handbook

Pioneer Clubs

Writers
Beth Almquist
Joyce Gibson
Susan Gilliland
Karen Leet
Jody Maas
Lucinda Rollings
Carol Smith

Editors
Rebecca M. Allen-Powell
Susan N. C. Price

Designer
Larry Taylor, Larry Taylor Design, Ltd.

Illustrators
Kevin Frank
Susan Waldrep
Michael Walker

Cover Design
Peter Schmidt, Granite Design

Curriculum Committee
Rebecca M. Allen-Powell
Judy Bryson
Virginia Patterson
Susan N. C. Price

Canadian Consultant
Jessica Breski

©2007 Pioneer Clubs®
PO Box 788, Wheaton, IL 60189-0788
630-293-1600
www.pioneerclubs.org

All rights reserved.
Except where noted, no part of this book may be reproduced in any form without written permission from Pioneer Clubs. Printed in USA.
References from the *King James Version* are identified (KJV).

Table of Contents

Introduction 4
Bible Awards 10
Growing in God's Way

- ☐ Using the Bible 10
- ☐ God's People 14
- ☐ Belonging to God 18
- ☐ Special to God 22
- ☐ Family Life 26
- ☐ God Made It All 30

Growing in God's Love

- ☐ God's Word 34
- ☐ Helping Others 38
- ☐ Loving God 42
- ☐ God and Me 46
- ☐ Honoring My Family 50
- ☐ Living God's Way 54

Growing Up in Jesus

- ☐ All About Church 58
- ☐ Friends Are Fun 61
- ☐ Good News 65
- ☐ Doing What's Right 70
- ☐ God Made Families 74
- ☐ Bible Teachings 78

Activity Awards 82
Arts and Communication

- ☐ Artist 82
- ☐ Bible Times 87
- ☐ Let's Pretend 91
- ☐ Making Music 94
- ☐ Story Fun 98

Myself, My Family, and Others

- [ ] Clothes **102**
- [ ] Club Helper **106**
- [ ] Cooking **110**
- [ ] Family Fun **114**
- [ ] Family Helper **118**
- [ ] Feeling Good **122**
- [ ] International Fun **126**
- [ ] Manners **131**
- [ ] Missions **135**
- [ ] My Friends **139**
- [ ] Parents **143**
- [ ] Safety First **147**

Hobbies and Projects

- [ ] Holidays **150**
- [ ] Nature Craft **154**
- [ ] Puppets **158**
- [ ] Puzzles **162**
- [ ] Science Fun **166**
- [ ] Stitch and Sew **171**
- [ ] Tools **174**

Outdoors and Camping

- [ ] Animals **178**
- [ ] Campfire 183
- [ ] Exploring 187
- [ ] Fishing **191**
- [ ] Our Earth 194
- [ ] Outdoors 197
- [ ] Trees **201**

Sports and Games

- [ ] Fitness Trail **206**
- [ ] Games 210
- [ ] Play Ball **214**
- [ ] Playing Together 218
- [ ] Relays **222**

Welcome to Pioneer Clubs!

Your club is called Voyagers. Voyagers do exciting things:
- **learn new skills**
- **learn to help and lead**
- **talk about God**
- **do favorite things**
- **find out how to live a life pleasing to Jesus**

Long ago, explorers sailed to our country. Their trip was called a voyage. They were called voyagers. They had adventures. They learned many new things. What they learned helped them be happy living in this new place.

Now men and women take trips into space. They are learning how to live in space. Their trips are called voyages, too.

In Pioneer Clubs, you will be on a special voyage. You will learn things to help you be happy. You will learn things that make God happy.

Draw a picture of yourself on a voyage. Draw yourself on a boat. Or draw yourself in a spaceship. Get ready to begin your Pioneer Clubs voyage!

How It All Began

Ask an adult to read you the story of how Pioneer Clubs began.

"There's nothing to do around here," complained 13-year-old Harriet Brehm and her friends in Winfield, Illinois. Their brothers had lots of fun in a boys club. So one day in 1939, Harriet asked Joe Coughlin, the boys' club leader, about starting a club for girls. Joe, a busy Wheaton College student, told Harriet, "If you can get a list of girls interested in club, I will find a leader."

A week later, Harriet saw "Uncle Joe" again. She excitedly said, "Here, I've got the list. When can we start?" Joe had no idea how to begin.

Many days passed with no word from Joe. So Harriet took things into her own hands. She called the college president. She told her story. A few hours later, Joe heard from the president: "If you promised those girls a leader, you need to find one."

Joe prayed hard. He asked the college newspaper to tell about his need for help. While he prayed, God talked to a college student named Betty Whitaker. She had been asking the Lord for a way to help young people Harriet's age. When she read the college paper, Betty knew it was God's answer.

A few weeks later, Harriet and her friends had their first club meeting. It was called Girls Guild. Soon college students started Girls Guild clubs in other towns.

Two years later, the club name changed to Pioneer Girls®, with activities built around the idea of pioneering and adventure. Soon clubs started for other ages.

Pioneer Girls' first office was in a china cabinet. But in the early 1940s, they found a proper office—and continued to grow. In 1981 Pioneer Girls changed its name to Pioneer Clubs and added boys clubs. Today, all 50 states and all Canadian provinces have club programs. There are even clubs in other countries around the world.

Thousands of young people before you have had exciting and rewarding experiences in Pioneer Clubs. We hope your years in club will be exciting and rewarding, too.

How to Join a Voyager Club

Joining your Voyager Club is easy.

First, you have to:
- be in first or second grade
- sign up with a club leader
- have a Bible and *Voyager Handbook* to use in club
- decide to come to club regularly

After doing these things, you may wear the Voyager Club crest. Color the picture of the crest when you have done all these things.

Second, learn some Pioneer Clubs facts:

- **Key Verse**

> "Thy word is a lamp unto my feet,
> and a light unto my path."
> (Psalm 119:105 KJV)

- **Aim**   That we may glorify the Lord Jesus.
- **Motto**   "Looking unto Jesus" (Hebrews 12:2a KJV)
- **Theme Song** (inside front cover)
- **Colors**   blue and red
- **Salute**   The salute is based on the key verse.
- **Logo**   The Pioneer Clubs logo is made up of an open Bible and a flame. The open Bible is the "light" that guides us in our life with Jesus. This special picture reminds us of the Pioneer Clubs theme verse.

"Thy word is a lamp | unto my feet, | and a light unto my path"

Third, yay, you're ready to be a Voyager! Fill in the blanks.

I Joined Voyagers at

_____
(church)

on _____
(date)

Voyager Club Meetings

In each meeting, you will work on a Bible award and activity award in your *Voyager Handbook.* You'll have fun playing games, doing skits, trying new skills, learning about God in Bible Explorations, and challenging yourself with Bible memory.

Your club may plan some special events. Look through your handbook. Talk to your club leader about activities you would like to try, such as:

- petting zoo visit
- holiday parties
- playground visit

Voyager Club Outfit

Use a Pioneer Clubs T-shirt as your club outfit. Your award display method may also be part of your club outfit. Your club leader will let you know what you can order through the Pioneer Clubs catalog.

What to Bring to Club Meetings

- *Voyager Handbook:* to work on Bible awards and activity awards.
- Bible: to learn about God.
- Shares: to help your club pay for special things.
- Snack: for eating! (Take your turn at bringing a snack.)
- Bible Memory Cards: from earlier weeks.

How to Earn Awards

Each Bible award or activity award has several steps. When you finish any part of an award, check it off in your book. When you finish all parts of an award, check it off in the Table of Contents, pages 2-3.

- **Bible Awards:** You will work on these in club.
- **Activity Awards:** Most activity awards will be done in club. Check with your club leader if you want to work on some at home. If you complete an award on your own, be sure you tell your club leader.

Extra Credit

Many activity awards have an Extra Credit part. You don't have to do the Extra Credit to earn the award. But if you do, you will receive a special gold star to put beside the award earned. When you do an Extra Credit, tell your club leader.

Highest Honor

To receive the Voyager Highest Honor pin:
- earn 18 Bible awards
- earn 20 activity awards
- do 15 Extra Credits

Bible Memory Help

Ask your club leader about using Voyager Bible Memory Packets. These are sets of Bible Memory Cards to help you review your verses at home. Have your leader choose the Bible Memory Packet that includes the Bible Memory Cards for the Bible awards you will be working on this year.

Your Club Leader

Your club leader is there to help you. Club leaders are special friends. Club leaders help you have fun. They help you earn awards. Best of all, they help you be good friends with Jesus.

How to Display Awards

Your club leader will choose a way to display awards. Include spots for the Pioneer Clubs logo crest, the Voyager crest, your membership pin, the bar patch, Bible awards and activity awards, Extra Credit stars, and the Highest Honor pin.

Camp Opportunities

Pioneer Clubs has a summer camping program called Camp Cherith®. The first Camp Cherith began in 1941. Today, there are Camp Cherith camps across the United States and Canada.

At camp you try new skills, meet new friends, and learn more about God. Camp Cherith has special awards you can only earn at camp. Ask your club leader to find out if you could go to camp next summer.

To learn about Camp Cherith in your area, visit **www.pioneerclubs.org** and click on "Camp Cherith." Or write to Camp Cherith, PO Box 788, Wheaton, IL 60189-0788, USA.

Your Pal

After you have been in Pioneer Clubs for a while, you may be given a Pal. A Pal is an adult from the church who will be your special friend and prayer partner. Ask your club leader about the Pal program at your church.

Using the Bible
BIBLE AWARD

To earn this award, do the things listed and check off each one.

1 God's Book

☐ **Part 1** Learn to use the Table of Contents.

The Bible is God's special message to you! You can learn to use it. Have someone show you how to find books using the Table of Contents.

Write down what page each book starts on:

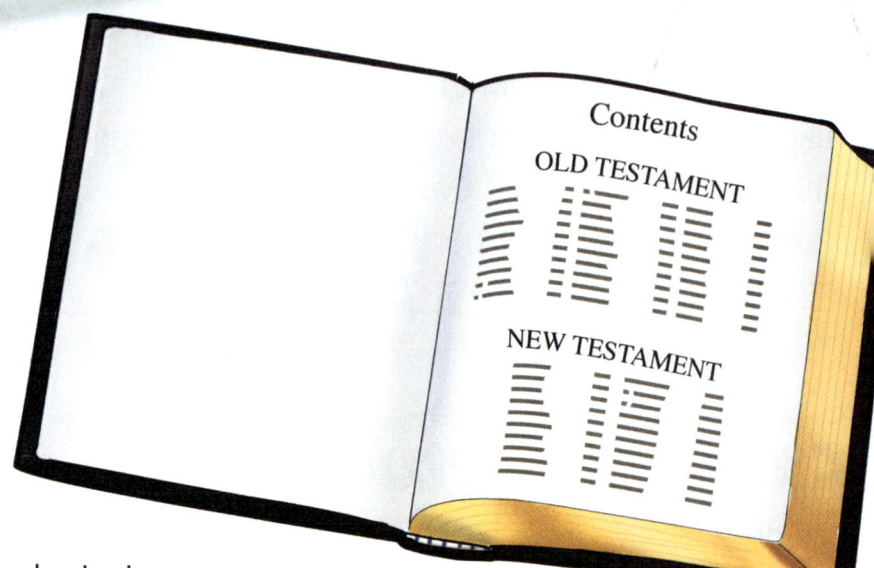

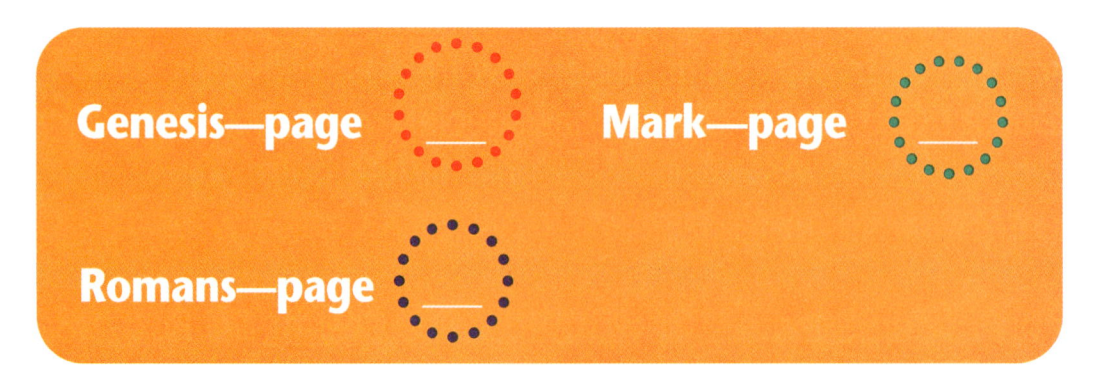

Genesis—page ___   **Mark—page** ___

Romans—page ___

☐ **Part 2** Learn to find verses.

Have someone show you how to find verses in the Bible. In the reference below, underline the book in green. Underline the chapter in red. Underline the verse number in blue.

Psalm 119:72

☐ **Part 3   Read God's rules.**

God gives us good rules in the Bible. Check off the verses as you find them. Ask a "Bible Buddy" to help. Circle the one you will work on obeying.

☐ Psalm 62:8

☐ Ephesians 6:1

☐ Exodus 20:15

2 When I'm Afraid

☐ **Part 1   Write a fear.**

Read or listen to Psalm 56:3. King David prayed this when he was afraid of his enemies. On an index card, write a word or draw a picture that stands for something you are afraid of.

☐ **Part 2   Make a magnet.**

On the other side of your index card, write out Psalm 56:3. Decorate the card. Stick a magnet on the back.

Hang your magnet where you will see it often. Pray David's prayer when you are afraid.

Psalm 56:3

3 God's Special Plan

☐ **Part 1 Old Testament and New Testament**

Match up the sentences.

The Old Testament tells what happened

The New Testament tells what happened

after Jesus was born on earth and after he went back to heaven.

before Jesus was born.

☐ **Part 2 A Good Prediction**

God helped the Old Testament writers write about Jesus. Read or listen to the last part of Isaiah 53:12. To see what the verse means, color in the spaces of the puzzle that have dots in them.

☐ **Part 3 Give Thanks**

Plan a way to thank God for one of these things:

- Telling the Bible writers what to write about Jesus.
- Sending Jesus to die and come back to life for you.

Circle how you will thank God:

Pray. **Draw.** **Sing.**

Your idea: _____

12

4 Keep Praying

☐ **Part 1** Decode the message.

Read or listen to Acts 18:1-7.

Find the important lesson by crossing out all of these letters: Q X Z

QNXXEZQVEZXRQ XSTZZOXQP PQXRAYXZZIZNQZQG.

☐ **Part 2** Spend time with God.

It's good to have a regular time to read the Bible and pray. Check off a good time for you. Ask your Bible Buddy to help you, if you want. God loves to hear from you!

My Choice

☐ First thing in the morning

☐ After school

☐ Before bed

☐ Some other time: _____

Memory Verses   ☐ Deuteronomy 6:6   ☐ Psalm 56:3-4a

When you learn a verse, put a Memory Verse Sticker on the back cover chart.

☐ This week I used my Bible Memory Cards to review my verses.

God's People
BIBLE AWARD

To earn this award, do the things listed and check off each one.

1 God Is with Me

☐ **Match the pictures.**

Read or listen to Joshua 1:8-9. Draw lines to the pictures on the right to complete the sentences. Put a check mark by one thing you want to remember this week. Pray that God will remind you about this.

Because God is always with me . . .

I will be **STRONG** at _____.

I will have [Have Courage!] at _____.

I will not be [😲] at _____.

I will trust [GOD] at _____.

I will obey [GOD] at _____.

Signed: _____
(my name)

school

home

play

night     day

2 I Can Choose Right

☐ **Part 1   Trust God and choose right.**

The spies God's people sent into Rahab's city needed to hide. Read or listen to Joshua 2:15-16 to see if Rahab hid them from her king's men.

Draw a way you will choose to do the right thing because you trust God.

☐ **Part 2   Trust God.**

Think about the promises and commands in Joshua 1:9. The sentences below repeat them. Circle those that make choosing the right thing easier for you.

Be strong and brave. Don't be afraid.

God is with us wherever we go.

Don't get discouraged.

15

3 Be a Witness

☐ **Part 1   True or false?**

Read or listen to Acts 1:8. Answer the following questions by circling "T" for True or "F" for False.

T or F (1)   Only pastors and Bible teachers can tell others about Jesus.

T or F (2)   Telling others about Jesus is our mission.

T or F (3)   The Holy Spirit gives us power to tell others about Jesus.

T or F (4)   We are to talk about Jesus only in our neighborhood.

T or F (5)   We are to talk about Jesus to friends.

Check the answers on page 17.

☐ **Part 2   Complete your mission.**

When you've told someone about Jesus this week, write the person's name here:

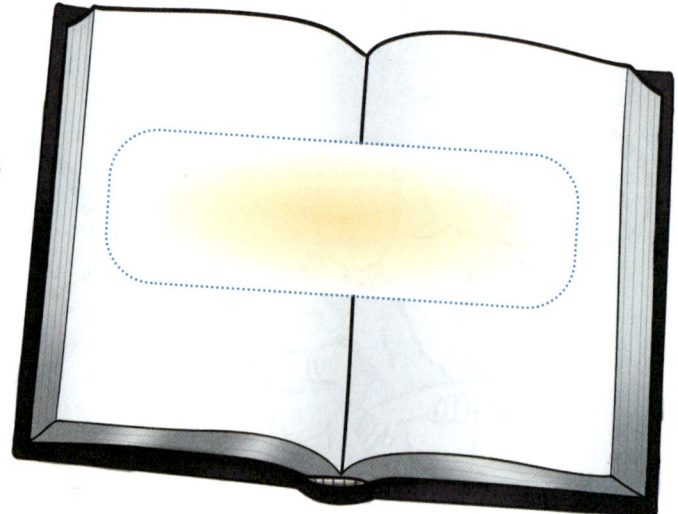

4 Be an Encourager

☐ **Part 1   Act out.**

Who is encouraging in each picture? With a friend, act out what happens for 1 picture. Circle the picture you do.

☐ **Part 2   Choose ideas.**

Draw a ☺ next to the pictures in Part 1 that show ways you will encourage someone this week. Or draw your own idea.

☐ **Part 3   Think about God**

Chapter 4 of Judges tells how Deborah encouraged Barak to trust that God would give the Israelites victory. Read or listen to Judges 4:23 to see what happened.

When God uses people to encourage you, what should you remember about God?

Answers to requirement 3, part 1:

1F, 2T, 3T, 4F, 5T

Memory Verses   ☐ Joshua 1:9b   ☐ Acts 1:8b

When you learn a verse, put a Memory Verse Sticker on the back cover chart.

☐ This week I used my Bible Memory Cards to review my verses.

17

Belonging to God
BIBLE AWARD

To earn this award, do the things listed and check off each one.

1 Praising My Shepherd

☐ **Part 1   See God as your shepherd.**

Read or listen to Psalm 23:1-6. King David says God is like a shepherd. Look at the pictures of the shepherd caring for the sheep. Connect each one with a picture of how God cares for your needs.

☐ **Part 2   Say thanks to God.**

David thanked God with a song. Circle a picture that shows how you will thank God for his care this week.

Or, draw your own idea:

18

2 Wandering from God

☐ **Part 1   Find the way to God!**

Read or listen to Isaiah 53:5-7. Read the sentences below. Follow the colored words and pictures through the maze.

> Sin is doing or thinking things that God does not like.

I'm like a 🐑 who runs away.

I sin against God my 🧔

Jesus died on the ✝ for my sin.

I can have peace with God!

☐ **Part 2   Show how you feel.**

Think about bad things you've thought or done this week. Inside the box, make a pencil mark for each one. Finish the first face to show how you feel.

Jesus died to pay for your sins. Erase the pencil marks! Finish the other face to show how you feel now.

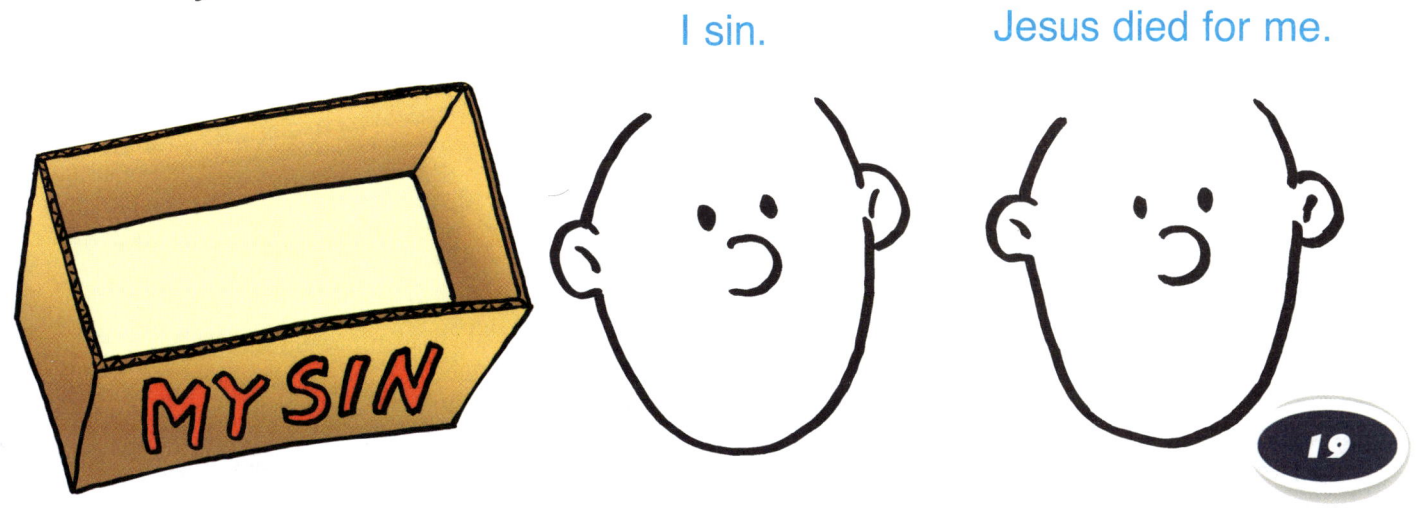

I sin.   Jesus died for me.

MY SIN

19

3 Trusting God's Care

☐ **Part 1   Tell the story!**

Elisha's friend had a problem. Did God care? Read or listen to 2 Kings 6:1-7 to find out. Then number the pictures in order.

☐ **Part 2   Tell your problem to God.**

God wants to do what's best for you. You can tell him about any problem, big or small. Draw a picture of a problem that you have. Or write it down. Pray about it.

Dear God, please help with...

4 Loving God and Others

☐ **Let God help.**

Read or listen to 1 John 4:11-14. It's not always easy to love others! But we can ask God to help. Think of 1 or 2 people who you can show love to. Write the names or draw their pictures below.

God, please help me love...

Memory Verses ☐ Psalm 23:1   ☐ Isaiah 53:6a

When you learn a verse, put a Memory Verse Sticker on the back cover chart.

☐ This week I used my Bible Memory Cards to review my verses.

Special to God
BIBLE AWARD

To earn this award, do the things listed and check o— each one.

1 God Made My Body

☐ **Part 1**   I am me.

What makes you different from everyone else? Make this person look more like you. Draw arrows to parts of your body that you are most thankful for.

☐ **Part 2**   God made me.

Circle one or more things you will do this week.

I will take care of the body God gave me by…

brushing my teeth.

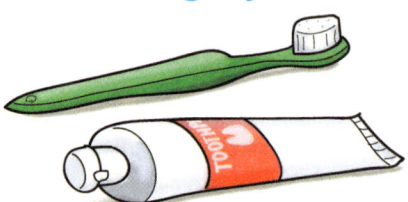

getting enough sleep.

running and playing.

eating good food.

My idea: _____

2 God Takes Care of Me

☐ **Read 1 Peter 5:7.**

To remind yourself to "throw" your troubles to God, make a "Worry Bag," like this. Put it somewhere that you'll see it every day.

When something worries you, write it on paper. Crumple the paper and throw it in the bag, praying to God to take that worry.

Remember that God can help you solve any problem.

3 God Makes Me His Child

☐ **Part 1   Choose a job.**

Read or listen to 1 John 3:1, 3-5. God loves you and wants to make you a part of his family! In his family, you have jobs. Check off at least 1 you will do.

God and Me

God, since I am part of your family, I will work at …

☐ asking you to help me do right.

☐ learning to be better by reading or listening to the Bible.

☐ staying away from bad things.

☐ asking you to forgive me for disobeying you.

_____
YOUR NAME

☐ **Part 2   Choose your answer.**

Maybe you are not part of God's family yet. Circle what you would like to do.

Ask Jesus to make me part of God's family.

Talk to this person about belonging to God's family: _____.

Something else: _____.

4 God Gives Me Talents

☐ **Part 1   What can I do well?**

Read 1 Kings 4:29-30. King Solomon wanted to rule well, so he asked for wisdom. He used the wisdom God gave him to be a wise ruler.

Start with something you might want to do. Draw a line to an ability that would help. Then circle a way you could honor God using that ability.

I want to:
- play in a band
- be a sports star
- write a book
- be a doctor
- design cars
- _____

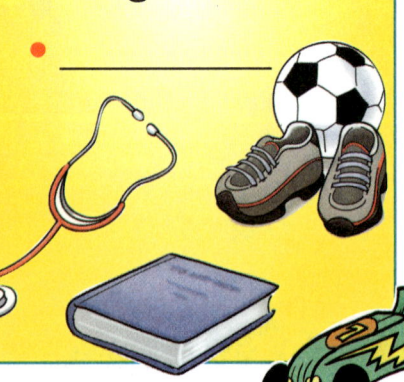

This ability would help:
- good at telling stories
- science skills
- drawing skills
- sports skills
- good at music
- _____

Then I could honor God by:
- writing skits for club
- making stuff for club
- helping heal people
- being a good sport
- making music in church
- _____

☐ **Part 2   With God's help I can…**
Write or draw to finish the sentence.

This week, I will use my ability for:

to help at club or church by doing this:

Memory Verses   ☐ Job 10:12a   ☐ 1 John 3:2a
When you learn a verse, put a Memory Verse Sticker on the back cover chart.
☐ This week I used my Bible Memory Cards to review my verses.

Family Life
BIBLE AWARD

To earn this award, do th[e] things listed and check o[ff] each one.

1 Showing Love

☐ **Part 1** Make a love list.

Read Ruth 1:16. God wants us to love family members just as Ruth loved Naomi. Circle the words that help you show love to your family. Cross out the words that do not help.

- Hugs
- Kisses
- Helping
- Getting even
- Kindness
- MEANNESS
- ARGUING
- Obeying
- Giving a compliment

☐ **Part 2** In My Home

Draw a picture in the house of a family member you will show love to this week. Put a ✱ by each idea in Part 1 that you will try.

2 Getting Along Together

☐ **Part 1   Unscramble.**

Read or listen to Ephesians 4:2. This verse tells good ways to act with your family. Use the clues and the verse to unscramble the 3 words below.

meluhb   ___ ___ ___ ___ ___ ___   Clue: **Not stuck-up**

teleng   ___ ___ ___ ___ ___ ___   Clue: **Not rough**

anettip   ___ ___ ___ ___ ___ ___ ___   Clue: **Can wait for things**

☐ **Part 2   I can be ...**

Draw a way you can be humble, gentle, or patient at home:

3 Feeling Envy

☐ **Part 1   Happy Face, Sad Face**

Cut eyeholes in a paper plate. On one side, draw a happy face. On the other side, draw a sad face.

☐ **Part 2   Good Choice, Bad Choice**

Read Joshua 7:10-12, 20. All the army of Israel suffered because Achan made a bad choice when he was envious.

You can learn to make good choices when you are envious.

Show whether you think these are good or bad choices by putting on your happy or sad mask. Then draw a happy or sad face by each idea.

A. Let the air out of your brother's great new bike's tires so he can't ride it.

B. Your older sister just got a fancy new computer. Ask nicely if she will help you use it sometime.

C. Cry and complain so your parents will give you shoes like your friend Cory has.

If an idea is a bad choice, think of a good one.

4 Looking for the Good

☐ **Part 1   Make stars.**

David went to visit his brothers in the army. He took them food. Read or listen to 1 Samuel 17:28. Circle which Eliab did.

Said thank you for the food.

Accused his brother of sneaking off to see the army and get out of work.

Make stars to help you do better than Eliab at seeing good things about your family members.

Write a family member's name on each star. Write 1 or 2 words to remind yourself of something good about that person.

☐ **Part 2   Hang the stars.**

Glue the family stars on a poster. Tell your family what good things you see in them.

GOOD THINGS ABOUT MY FAMILY

- DAD READS
- KELLY PLAYS GAMES

Memory Verses   ☐ Ruth 1:16b   ☐ Ephesians 4:2

When you learn a verse, put a Memory Verse Sticker on the back cover chart.

☐ This week I used my Bible Memory Cards to review my verses.

God Made It All
Bible Award

To earn this award, do the things listed and check off each one.

1 God's Wonderful World

☐ **Take care of God's world.**

Read or listen to Psalm 104:10-17 and 24.
Circle ways of showing thanks for things God has made.
Cross out things that hurt what God has made.

30

2 Animal Review

☐ **Part 1   I will take care.**

Read or listen to Psalm 104:18-28. God takes care of the animals he made. He wants us to help, too.

Give a star to each person who is caring for an animal.

☐ **Part 2   Feed the birds.**

Have an adult poke two holes in the side of an empty plastic margarine tub for you. Thread string through the holes and tie it in a loop for a hanger.

Mix peanut butter and birdseed. Use mostly seeds so you get a stiff mixture. Press the mix into the plastic tub. Press some raisins or dried cranberries into the top. Hang the tub outside and watch for birds to come and feed.

3 God Cares

☐ **Part 1 Trust God's care.**

On the day side, draw something you do each day. On the night side, draw something you do each night.

Day and Night God Cares for Me

☐ **Part 2 Praise God for caring.**

This week, remember to praise God because he cares for you.

If you plan to praise him in the daytime, circle the day picture. If you will praise him for his care at night, circle that picture.

4 God Is in Charge

☐ **Part 1   Find God's promise.**

Have someone tell you the story of Noah's Ark. Read or listen to Genesis 9:12-15. What does God promise?

Color the picture. Draw the sign of God's promise.

☐ **Part 2   Remember that God's in charge.**

Noah knew that God is in charge of everything. He said, "Yes, God, I will obey you!" Draw a line to finish what *you* will say to God.

Thank you   follow your ways.

I will do   for your promise and your rainbows.

I want to   what you want me to do.

Memory Verses   ☐ Psalm 104:24   ☐ Psalm 121:2

When you learn a verse, put a Memory Verse Sticker on the back cover chart.

☐ This week I used my Bible Memory Cards to review my verses.

God's Word
BIBLE AWARD

To earn this award, do the things listed and check off each one.

1 Honor God's Word

☐ **Part 1**   Discover how God gave his message.

Read or listen to Deuteronomy 10:3-5. God gave the Ten Commandments to Moses. They are God's message to us, too. Number the events in the right order.

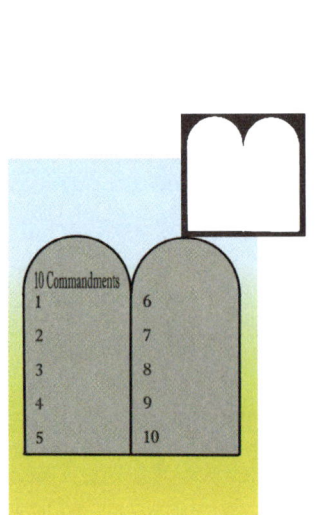

☐ **Part 2**   Tell what you will do.

Now that you know that the Bible is God's message to you, what will you do? Make a bookmark that shows what you will do. *Ideas:*

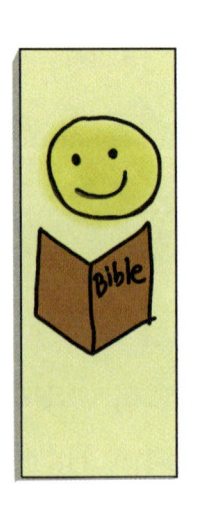

2 Keep It in Your Heart

☐ **Part 1** Learn how to find verses.

Have someone teach you how to find books, chapters, and verses in the Bible. Practice on Matthew 4:4. Draw lines to match the parts of the reference below with what they tell you.

MATTHEW 4 : 4

| this is the verse | this is the book | this is the chapter |

☐ **Part 2** Choose good locks.

Read or listen to Matthew 4:4. Jesus meant that we need the Bible. It's like a treasure. Circle the ways that would help you "lock" a Bible verse into your memory.

- Hear the verse.
- Read the verse.
- Say the verse aloud.
- Sing the verse.
- Think about the words.
- Play a game with the verse.
- Make up motions for the words.
- Love the words.

☐ **Part 3** Memorize.

Color the locks you will use to memorize at least one of these verses. Be sure to memorize the reference, too.

☐ Psalm 118:1   ☐ Psalm 4:3b   ☐ Isaiah 26:4

3 Follow the Bible Path

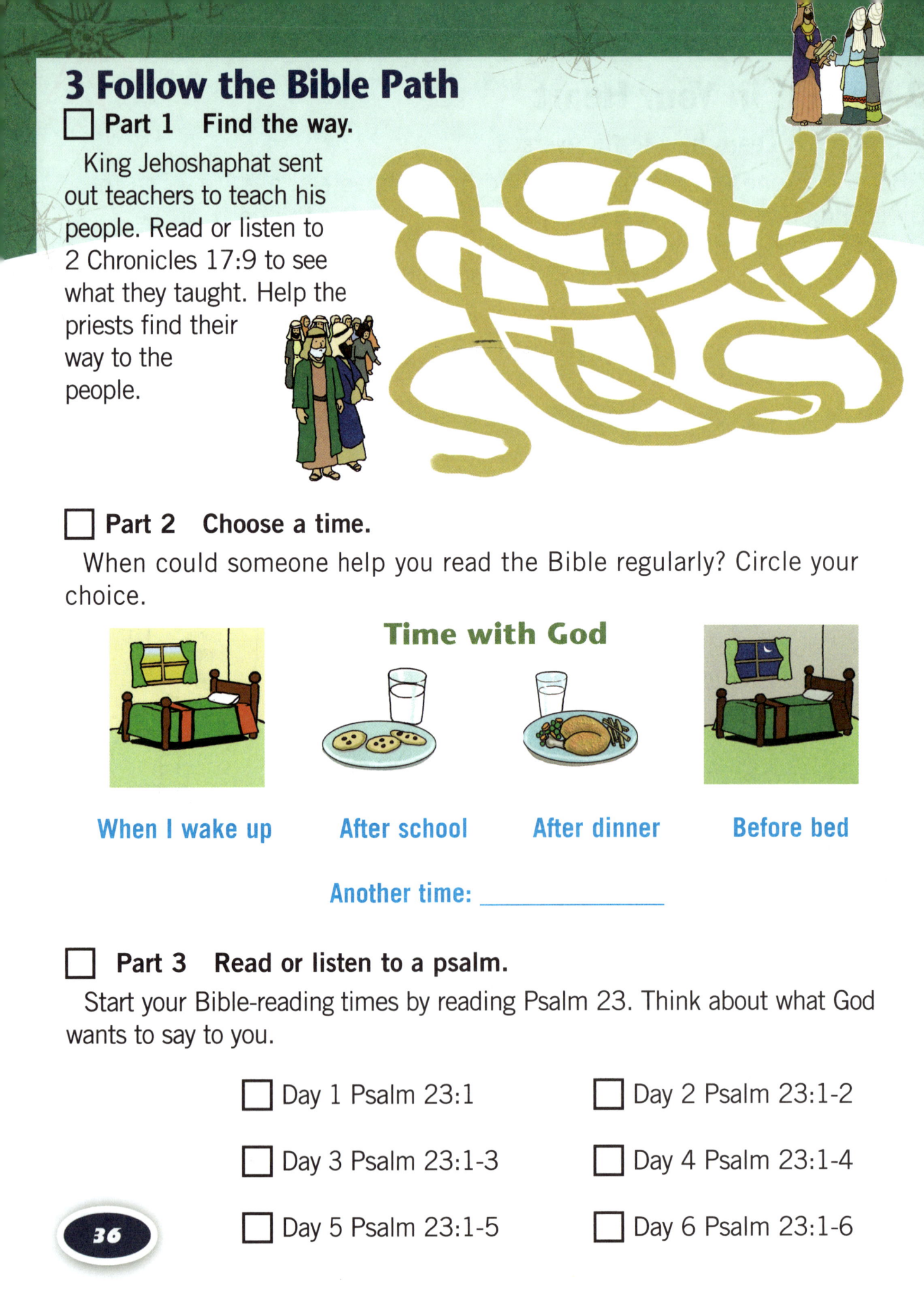

☐ **Part 1   Find the way.**

King Jehoshaphat sent out teachers to teach his people. Read or listen to 2 Chronicles 17:9 to see what they taught. Help the priests find their way to the people.

☐ **Part 2   Choose a time.**

When could someone help you read the Bible regularly? Circle your choice.

Time with God

When I wake up   **After school**   **After dinner**   **Before bed**

Another time: _____

☐ **Part 3   Read or listen to a psalm.**

Start your Bible-reading times by reading Psalm 23. Think about what God wants to say to you.

☐ Day 1 Psalm 23:1   ☐ Day 2 Psalm 23:1-2

☐ Day 3 Psalm 23:1-3   ☐ Day 4 Psalm 23:1-4

☐ Day 5 Psalm 23:1-5   ☐ Day 6 Psalm 23:1-6

4 Check It Out

☐ **Part 1   See what the Bible says.**

Read or listen to Acts 17:10-12. The Bereans used the Bible to see if what they heard was true. You can, too. Match each picture with a Bible verse that would help you know if the friend's idea is true.

Treat others as you would like to be treated. (Luke 6:31)

Do not lie. (Leviticus 19:11)

Do not steal. (Exodus 20:15)

- forgot to do my homework.
- It's okay to tell the teacher you were sick.
- I found that kid's new pen on the floor.
- It's okay to keep it. Finders keepers, losers weepers.
- That kid called me a bad name.
- It's okay to call him a bad name then.

☐ **Part 2 Use the Bible.**

Circle how you will use the Bible when you need to know if something is true.

- What does the Bible say about that?
- Think of a memory verse that fits.
- Ask someone to help you read what the Bible says about it.
- My idea:

Memory Verses   ☐ Deuteronomy 10:4a   ☐ Matthew 4:4

When you learn a verse, put a Memory Verse Sticker on the back cover chart.

☐ This week I used my Bible Memory Cards to review my verses.

Helping Others
BIBLE AWARD

To earn this award, do the things listed and check o each one.

"**ANYONE** can be my neighbor."

1 My Neighbors

☐ **Part 1** Connect the dots.

Read or listen to Luke 10:25-37. Who would Jesus say are your neighbors? Connect the dots. Color the pictures.

38

☐ **Part 2   Plan to be a good neighbor.**

Think of someone who needs your help or kindness. Circle something you will do for that person this week. Ask God to help you.

Help.   Share.   Be friendly.   Give.

My idea: _____

2 Serving Each Other

☐ **Part 1   Finish the pictures.**

Read or listen to Mark 10:43-44. Look at each picture of someone being selfish. Finish the other picture to show that person serving instead.

☐ **Part 2   Serve others right now!**

Work with your club or family to help someone. Draw what you did.

39

3 Special Needs

☐ **Part 1 Find what's different.**

Read or listen to Mark 10:51-52. Only God can heal people. But you can care like Jesus and try to help.

How are these 2 pictures different? Find 5 special needs or problems in the first picture. In the other picture, who helped? How?

☐ **Part 2 Be a helper.**

Think of a way you could help someone with special needs this week. Circle that part of the second picture, or write your idea below.

40

4 Telling Others

☐ **Share good news.**

Read or listen to Mark 7:31-37. Who was excited to tell others about Jesus?

You can tell what you know about Jesus, too. Here are ideas. Find the purple words to the right in the puzzle. Circle an idea that you will tell someone this week, or draw your own.

Jesus **hears** prayers.

Jesus **died** for you.

Jesus **loves** you.

Jesus **gives** you what you need.

Jesus **did** something for me!

```
Q R D I E D N Z
P X Z J V A W X
H E A R S Z U I
R L U V Z G X Q
M O X C D I D Z
W V M T Q V S Y
Z E W H X E M M
Y S Q Y W S Q X
```

My idea

Memory Verses   ☐ Luke 10:27b   ☐ Mark 10:45

When you learn a verse, put a Memory Verse Sticker on the back cover chart.

☐ This week I used my Bible Memory Cards to review my verses.

Loving God
BIBLE AWARD

To earn this award, do the things listed and check off each one.

1 God Is My Helper

☐ **Part 1** See how God helps.

Have someone tell you the story of Moses and the escape from Egypt. Read or listen to Exodus 14:13-14. God helped the Israelites and he helps you, too! To find out how, match up the pictures with the sentences.

God helps me learn how to live when I read the _____.

God helps me by giving me _____ to take care of me.

God helps me by listening when I _____.

God helps me not to _____.

God _____ me.

PRAY

WORRY

LOVES

BIBLE

HELPFUL ADULTS

42

☐ **Part 2 Ask God for help.**

What do you need help with? You can ask God for help because he loves you! Every time you ask God for help this week, check off a praying picture. Every time you thank him when he helps you, check off a cheering picture.

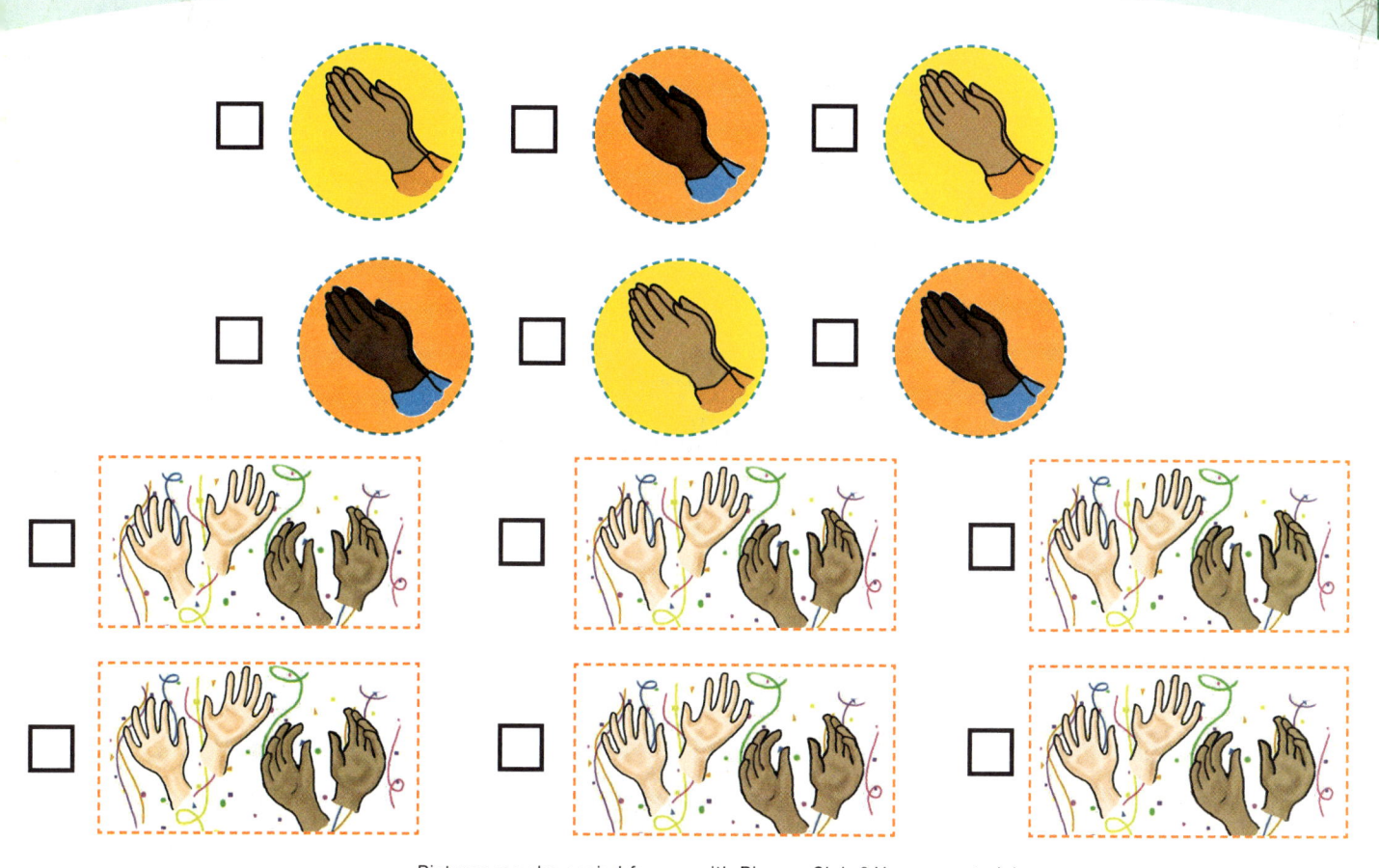

Pictures may be copied for use with Pioneer Clubs® Voyager materials.

2 God's Gift

☐ **Part 1 Find a free gift.**

Read or listen to Romans 6:23.

1. Draw a big, bold X through the phrase that this verse says you have done.

2. Draw a 🎁 around the free gift God will give you.

3. Circle something you can do this week to thank God for his gift.

life forever   **pray**   **disobeyed God**

try to obey God   **read the Bible**

43

☐ **Part 2 Finish the prayer.**

Circle one or more faces to show how you want to finish the prayer.

Dear Jesus, I know I have disobeyed you…

Please come into my life.

I'm not sure what to do now.

I've already asked you to be part of my life. Thank you!

3 Showing My Love

☐ **Choose ways.**

Read or listen for what Jesus says in Luke 10:25-28. We can show our love for God in many ways. Color some you will do this week.

4 Trusting God

☐ **Draw a picture.**

A Bible-times man, Daniel, was thrown to the lions for doing something good—praying to God. But he trusted God. Read or listen to what God did in Daniel 6:21-22.

God, help me trust you at this time…

Draw a picture of a time when you need to trust God. Pray the prayer at the top of your picture.

Memory Verses ☐ Exodus 15:2a ☐ John 3:16

When you learn a verse, put a Memory Verse Sticker on the back cover chart.

☐ This week I used my Bible Memory Cards to review my verses.

45

God and Me
Bible Award

To earn this award, do the things listed and check off each one.

1 God Made Me

☐ **Part 1   Show how you feel.**

God made you. He knew you before you were born. He loves you! Read or listen to what God said in the first part of Jeremiah 1:5.

Draw or write how you feel about God.

☐ **Part 2   Say thanks!**

What can you do to say thanks to God for making you and knowing you? Show an adult what you would do.

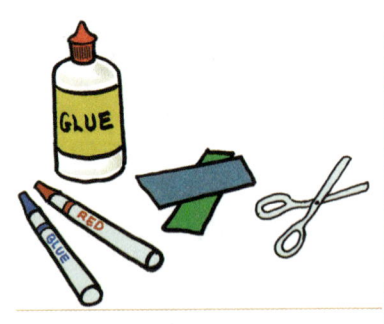

Make a card.

Pray to him.

Sing a song to him.

My idea

2 God Takes Care of Me

☐ **Part 1** God cares.

Match the things and people God created to the ways God shows care for them.

Flowers and trees need water.

Children need clothing.

People get sick.

Birds need food.

Pets need food.

Pet owners feed their pets.

Doctors and nurses help sick people get better.

Plants grow seeds and fruit.

Parents buy or make clothing.

Clouds bring rain.

☐ **Part 2** I can do this.

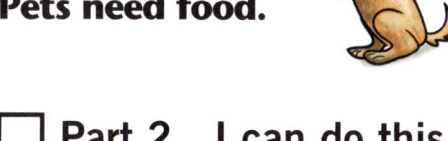

Read Matthew 6:33. God wants us to think about knowing him and following him. Color what you might do when you're worried about something. Cross out what you shouldn't do.

Just keep worrying.

Pray about my worries.

Pretend I'm not worried.

Whatever! I don't care!

Read about how God cares for me.

Talk with a parent.

47

3 Jesus Loves Me

☐ **Part 1 Do a dot-to-dot.**

Read or listen to Mark 10:13-14, 16. Follow the dots. What did you draw? Who loves you?

☐ **Part 2 Come to Jesus.**

Jesus wants you to come to him. Look at this maze. Use the clues on it to find your way to Jesus.

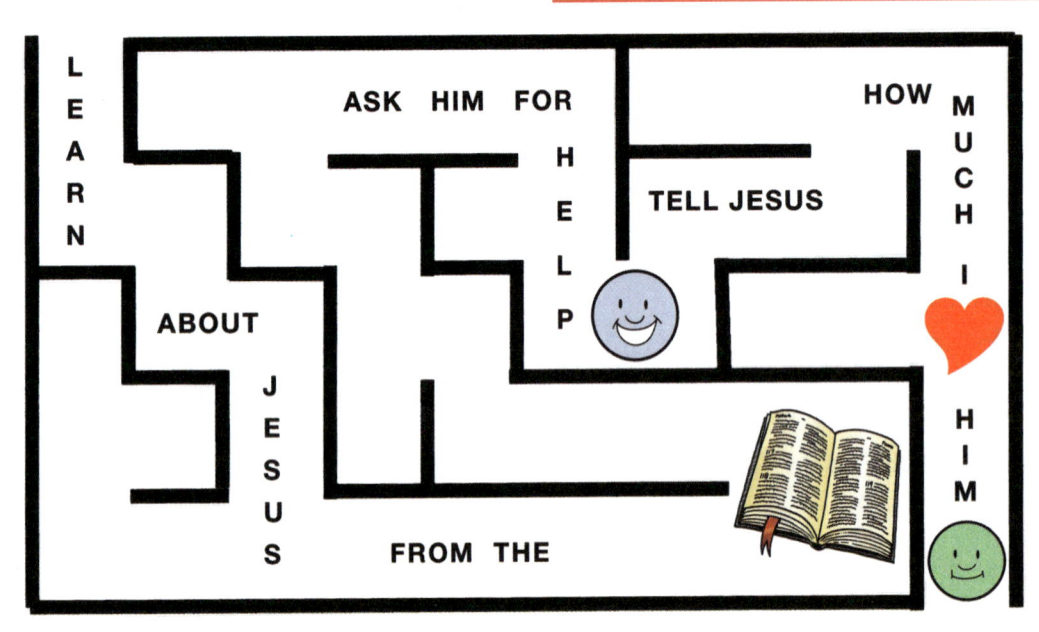

Maze clues: LEARN ABOUT JESUS FROM THE ASK HIM FOR HELP TELL JESUS HOW MUCH I ♥ HIM

JESUS

4 God Guides Me

☐ **Part 1 Make good choices.**

Cross out bad choices in these pairs of pictures.

48

Act out or tell an adult a good choice for 1 of these as well:

- A friend wants to play but you have been told to clean your room.

- You are hungry but you've been told not to have any snacks before dinner.

- You forgot to let the puppy out and now there's a puddle on the floor.

☐ **Part 2   Ask God.**

Draw a picture about a choice you need to make. Pray for God to guide you.

Keep praying if you don't understand God's answer right away.

Here's how many times I prayed this week:

1   2   3   4   5   6   7   more

Memory Verses   ☐ Jeremiah 1:5a   ☐ Mark 10:14b

When you learn a verse, put a Memory Verse Sticker on the back cover chart.

☐ This week I used my Bible Memory Cards to review my verses.

Honoring My Family
BIBLE AWARD

To earn thi[s] award, do t[he] things liste[d] and check [off] each one.

1 Forgiveness

☐ **Part 1   Why forgive?**

Read or listen to Colossians 3:13b. On the chart, cross out all of these letters: A, B, C, H, L, N, P, U, and T. Write the leftover letters in order on the blanks below the chart.

B	C	P	G	O	H	D	B	F
A	H	L	O	U	A	U	R	L
G	I	U	A	C	V	E	A	A
S	N	M	T	H	E	L	T	P

WHY FORGIVE?

God _Forgives_ _us_

☐ **Part 2 I can forgive.**

What steps can you take to forgive? Put the pictures below in order by drawing a line from each picture to a step.

Step 3

Step 2

Step 1

remember Jesus forgives me

forgive

pray

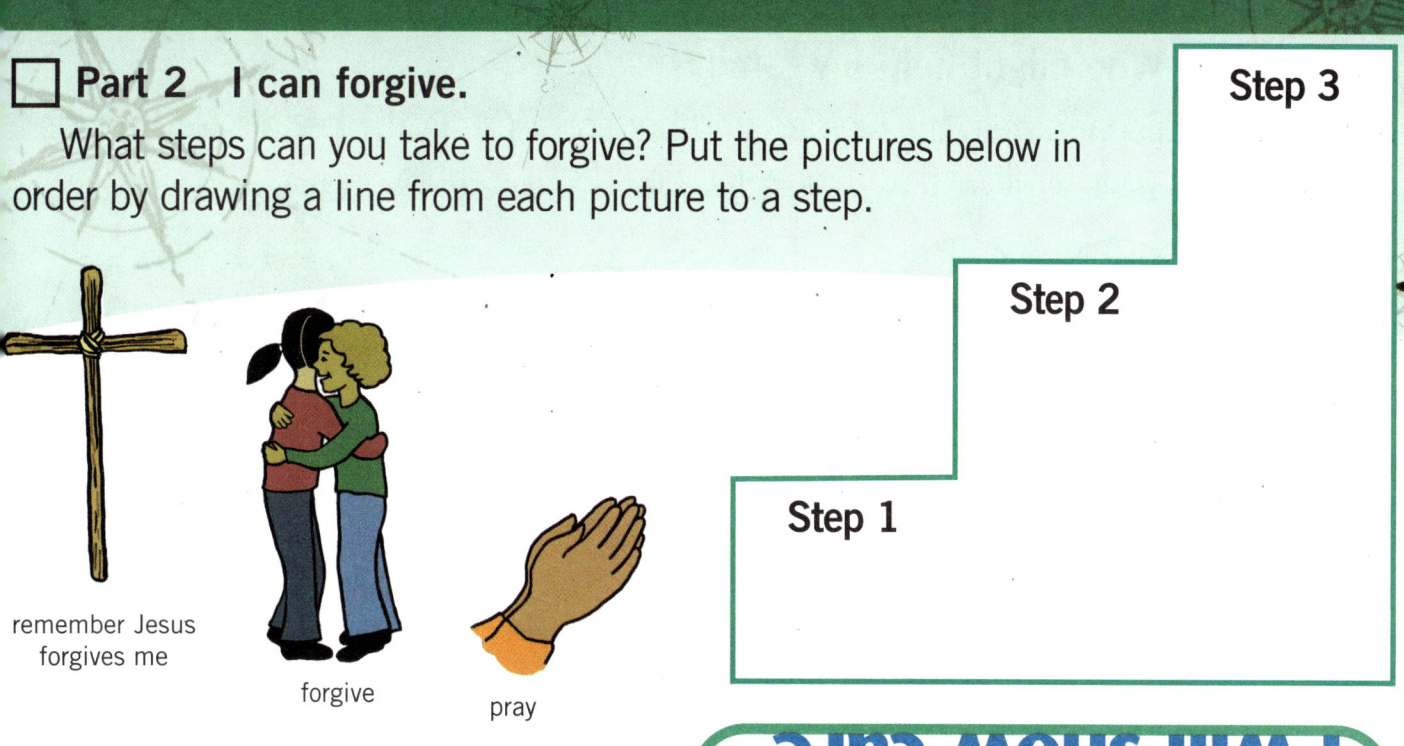

☐ **Part 3 I will forgive.**

In the third step above, write the name of a family member you will try to forgive this week.

2 Caring About Parents

☐ **I will care.**

Read or listen to Colossians 3:12. Draw 1 way you will show care this week to your mom or dad or another special person who takes care of you.

I will show care

3 God Helps Families

☐ **Part 1 Finish the faces.**

Read or listen to 2 Kings 4:1-7. Fill in the faces.

Show how the mom might have felt in verse 4.

Show how the mom felt in verse 7.

51

☐ **Part 2   Who might help my family?**

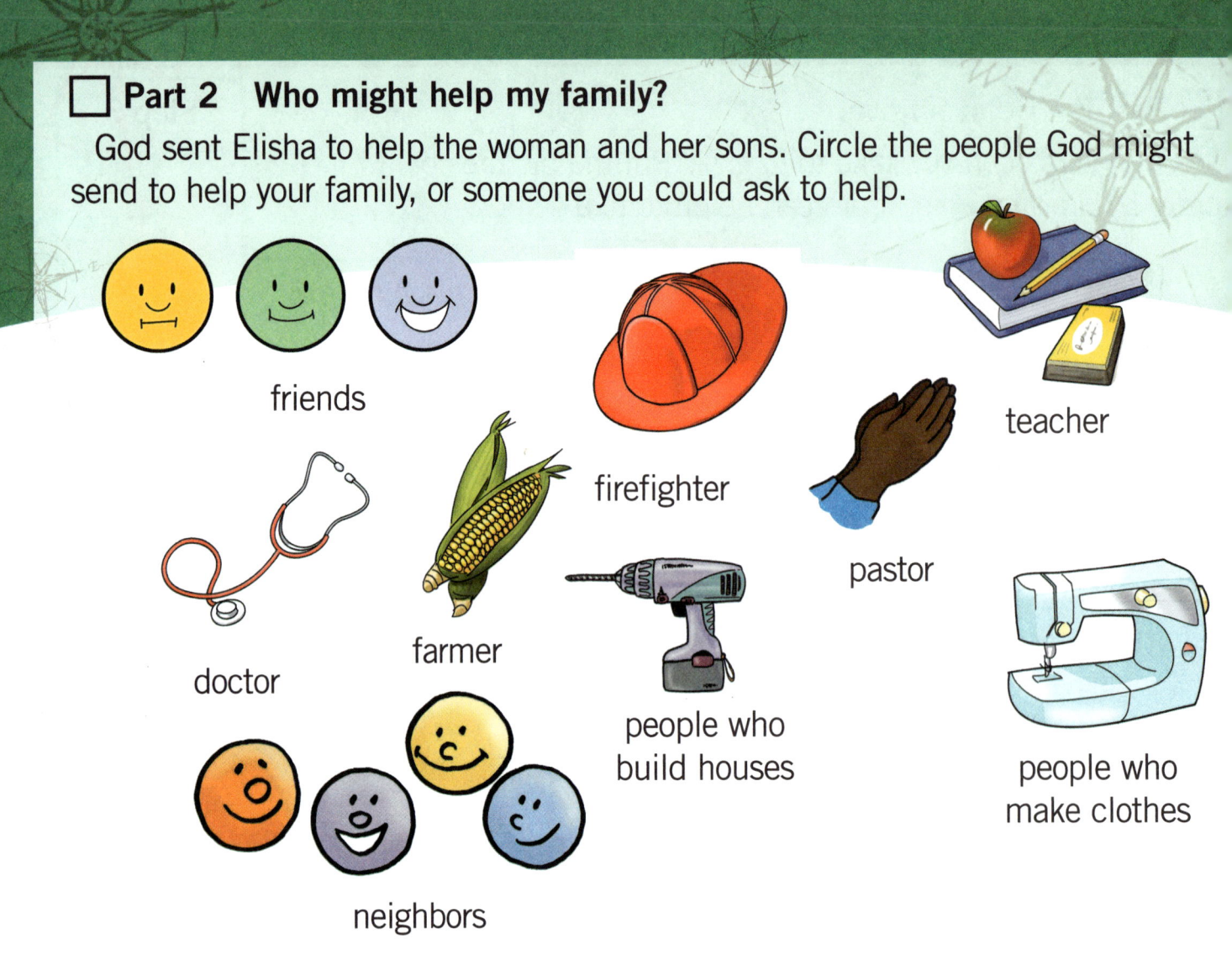

God sent Elisha to help the woman and her sons. Circle the people God might send to help your family, or someone you could ask to help.

friends

doctor

farmer

firefighter

people who build houses

pastor

teacher

people who make clothes

neighbors

☐ **Part 3   Remember to say thanks.**

Check each day you thank God for helping your family.

SUNDAY	MONDAY	TUESDAY	WEDNESDAY	THURSDAY	FRIDAY	SATURDAY

Chart may be copied for use with Pioneer Clubs® Voyager materials.

Or put a star by someone in Part 2 who you will talk to this week about a problem in your family.

4 Helping My Family

☐ **Part 1   Order the pictures.**

Read or listen to Exodus 1:22 and 2:1-10. Put these pictures in order by numbering them from 1-5.

This woman can care for the baby.

1

☐ **Part 2   Act out chores.**

Miriam helped her family. God is pleased when we help! Act out chores you could do to help your family. Have someone guess what you are doing. Think of chores you don't usually do.

Memory Verses   ☐ Colossians 3:13b   ☐ Colossians 3:12a

When you learn a verse, put a Memory Verse Sticker on the back cover chart.

☐ This week I used my Bible Memory Cards to review my verses.

53

Living God's Way
BIBLE AWARD

To earn this award, do the things listed and check o[ff] each one.

1 Being a Light

☐ **Part 1** Read this puzzle.

Color the dotted shapes with your favorite color. Color the shapes without dots black.

When I shine my light, people will...

☐ **Part 2** Shine your light!

Read or listen to Matthew 5:14-16. Draw rays of light out to show the things you'll do this week to be like light in your world.

Help

Be mean

Be kind

Fight

Pray

Smile

Share

2 Walking with God

☐ **What will you do?**

Read or listen to Genesis 6:5, 9, 22. All the people around Noah were mean and bad. But even so, Noah walked with God—he loved God and obeyed him. God rewarded him for this.

Draw a picture of yourself walking with God this week, using one of the ideas here.

Tell the truth. Don't play favorites. Do a good job at school. Be kind. Obey parents. Do my best to get along with others.

3 Keeping Friends

☐ **Part 1   What is different?**

Read or listen to Proverbs 15:18. Circle 8 things that are different in the second picture. Which picture shows a good way to handle a disagreement with a friend?

"You're not my friend anymore!"

"Let's still be friends and work out our differences."

☐ **Part 2   Make a plan.**

Write the names of 1 or 2 friends.

_____

_____

What is your plan for the next time you have a disagreement? Cross out the things you won't do.

MY PLAN

◀ Be patient.

Decide to work things out. ▶

◀ Yell.

Decide to still be friends. ▶

◀ Forgive.

Call names. ▶

4 Being Honest

☐ **Part 1 Think of reasons.**

Read or listen to Luke 22:54-57. Peter was afraid to tell the truth. Act out for friends how you could encourage a friend to tell the truth if these things happened.

You did WHAT?
Your friend did something that might mean big trouble.

TEST You need to study more!
Your friend isn't doing well in school.

ha, ha!
Others might laugh if your friend tells the truth.

☐ **Part 2 Decide to obey.**

Unscramble the words.

Word List

Remember Jesus **ELSOV** _____ me no matter what.

Remember Jesus **SNAWT** _____ me to tell the truth.

Ask Jesus for **PHLE** _____.

CERPICAT _____ being truthful with a friend.

practice

loves

help

wants

Read the sentences. Think of another idea to help you want to obey God and tell the truth.

My idea: _____

Memory Verses   ☐ Matthew 5:14a   ☐ Genesis 6:9b

When you learn a verse, put a Memory Verse Sticker on the back cover chart.

☐ This week I used my Bible Memory Cards to review my verses.

All About Church
Bible Award

To earn this award, do the things listed and check off each one.

1 Church Is for Worship

☐ **Part 1 Why Worship?**

Unscramble the reasons why worshiping God is good.

God does **teagr** _____ things for us.

Worshiping **sleph** _____ us **voel** _____ God more.

God **lsetl** _____ us to worship.

It's a way to **tnahk** _____ God.

WORD LIST

love

tells

thank

great

helps

☐ **Part 2 Worship in Church**

Do 1 of these things this week:

____ Help plan a worship time in club. Include at least:
- 2 songs. Name of 1 song:

  _____

- 1 prayer

____ Ask an adult to take you to church. Write or draw what you like best about church.

2 Encouraging Others at Church

☐ **Be an encourager.**

Read Acts 4:36. Join the Barnabas team! Cut out and color a happy face. Give it to someone at church or Pioneer Clubs as encouragement. Tell that person you will pray for him or her. Color a happy face here when you pray.

3 Church Tells About Jesus

☐ **Part 1 Come and hear.**

Read Acts 5:42. People come to church to learn about Jesus. Draw a picture of yourself learning about Jesus in church or Pioneer Clubs.

☐ **Part 2 Bring a friend.**

Can you invite a friend to church? Or to Pioneer Clubs? You can both learn about Jesus. Who can you bring? Write a name or initial here:

Vincent/Tyler/Enreagayen

4 Churches Help People

☐ **Part 1 Learn how to give.**

Read or listen to 2 Corinthians 9:7. Churches help people by giving. Show your club leader or parent how you should act when you're helping your church give to people.

Finish this face to show how God wants us to feel about giving.

☐ **Part 2 Give a gift.**

With your club or family, collect gifts to give to a homeless shelter. *Ideas:*

Or have your club leader or parent help you choose and do another giving project.

Memory Verses ☐ Psalm 100:2   ☐ Acts 5:42b

When you learn a verse, put a Memory Verse Sticker on the back cover chart.

☐ This week I used my Bible Memory Cards to review my verses.

Friends Are Fun
BIBLE AWARD

To earn this award, do the things listed and check off each one.

Helping a Friend

☐ **Read or listen to Proverbs 17:17a.**

Do the maze to find ideas of things to help friends with. Circle 1 thing you will help a friend with this week.

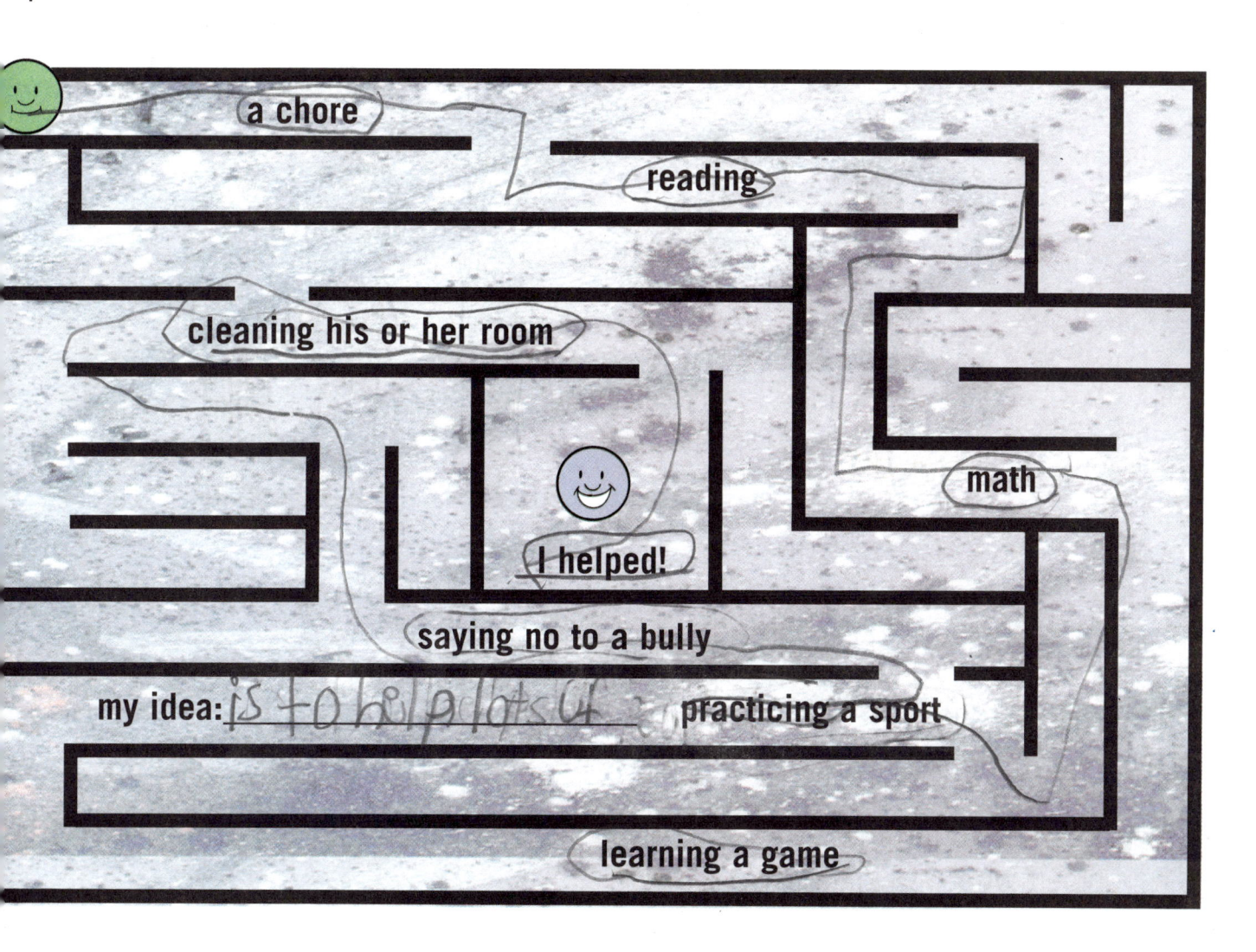

- a chore
- reading
- cleaning his or her room
- math
- I helped!
- saying no to a bully
- practicing a sport
- learning a game

my idea: is to help lots of

61

2 Being a Friend

☐ **Part 1** Think of better ways.

Read or listen to 2 Samuel 9:6-7. David was a good friend to Jonathan. He decided to be a good friend to Jonathan's son, Mephibosheth, too. For each picture, tell someone how to be a good friend. Or act it out.

I wish I could do that.

It was an accident!

I can be kind.

I can be generous.

May we play?

I can be brave.

☐ **Part 2** Choose a way.

Think of a way you can be a kind or brave or generous friend this week. Draw something to remind yourself what you will do.

☐ **Part 3 Ask God.**

God is the best friend you can have. Talk to God and ask him to help you be a good friend. You may use 1 of these prayers or make up your own.

> God, please help me be a good friend.

> God, thank you for loving me. Help me love my friends.

3 Forgiving Others

☐ **Part 1   Act out a story.**

Read or listen to Matthew 18:21-33. Act out the story with family or friends. Circle the part you played.

God forgives us for a lot when we ask. He wants us to forgive our friends.

King · servant who owed a lot · servant who owed a little · another servant

☐ **Part 2   Forgive a friend.**

Think of a friend who needs your forgiveness. Circle the ways you can forgive.

- Pray that Jesus would help me forgive.
- Say, "I forgive you."
- Write a note that lets my friend know we're still friends.
- My idea: I fogivess my sis

Write your friend's name on the line. Talk to Jesus.

63

4 Welcoming Others!

☐ **Part 1** Do a puzzle.

Read or listen to 2 Kings 4:8-10. The woman was welcoming to Elisha. Find the underlined words in the puzzle to see how you can be welcoming to friends.

WORD LIST
be polite
be kind
share
give
love
take turns

```
Q G X Z M B L
K I N D E W O
Y V Z W C C V
Q E S H A R E
Z P O L I T E
X C T U R N S
K W X A Z B C
```

☐ **Part 2** Invite a friend.

Find a way to make someone welcome. *Some ideas:*
- Invite someone to Pioneer Clubs.
- Ask someone to play with you at lunch or after school.
- Invite someone to church or Sunday school.
- Invite someone to a school play or concert.

I will invite _____.

Make an invitation for your friend. Be welcoming!

Please come to Pioneer Clubs at Neighborhood Church with me. We meet on Wednesday nights at 6 p.m.

Memory Verses ☐ Proverbs 17:17a ☐ Psalm 65:3

When you learn a verse, put a Memory Verse Sticker on the back cover chart.

☐ This week I used my Bible Memory Cards to review my verses.

Good News
Bible Award

To earn this award, do the things listed and check off each one.

1 Jesus Loves Me

☐ **Part 1 Color the heart.**
Read or listen to Matthew 18:12-14. Color the heart that shows how the shepherd felt because of the one lost sheep.

☐ **Part 2 Unscramble.**
Who is our Shepherd? (UJESS.) Jesus

Why are we "lost"? (DSBIOEY.) We Disobey God.

☐ **Part 3 Choose your answers.**
Read or listen to John 3:16 and Romans 5:8. Color each heart that is true for *you*. Pray about those ideas.

- I know Jesus loves me.
- I know Jesus died for the bad things I've done.
- I love Jesus.
- I've already asked Jesus to forgive me for the bad things I've done.
- I want to ask Jesus to forgive me for the bad things I've done.
- I want to talk to someone more about this.

Hearts may be copied for use with Pioneer Clubs® Voyager materials.

2 Jesus Helps

☐ **Part 1** See how Jesus helped then.

Read or listen to Matthew 14:22-33. Peter was scared when he got out of the boat. Use these boating flags to fill in the blanks.

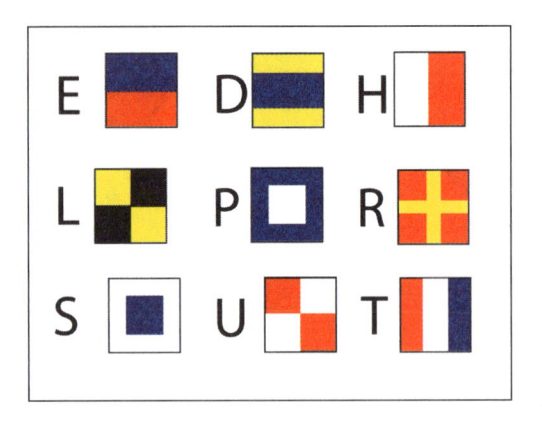

What did Peter forget to do?

__Trust__ **Jesus.**

What did Jesus do?

__Helped__ **Peter.**

☐ **Part 2** See how Jesus helps now.

Circle each picture where Jesus can help.

66

☐ **Part 3   Ask Jesus to help.**

Write a word or draw a picture to tell Jesus 1 thing you need help with.

Put a ✓ under each day you pray and ask Jesus' help.

| Sunday | Monday | Tuesday | Wednesday | Thursday | Friday | Saturday |

3 Follow Jesus

☐ **Part 1   Learn to follow.**

Read or listen to Mark 1:16-18. Find the underlined words in the puzzle to see how you can learn to follow Jesus. That means living Jesus' way.

Read the **Bible**
Pray
Listen in club and church
Talk to other Christians
Practice what the Bible says

```
Q Z O J Z B W X
P R A C T I C E
R X G L Q B M X
A F W T A L K J
Y J X M Z E D Q
X L I S T E N G
```

MORE →

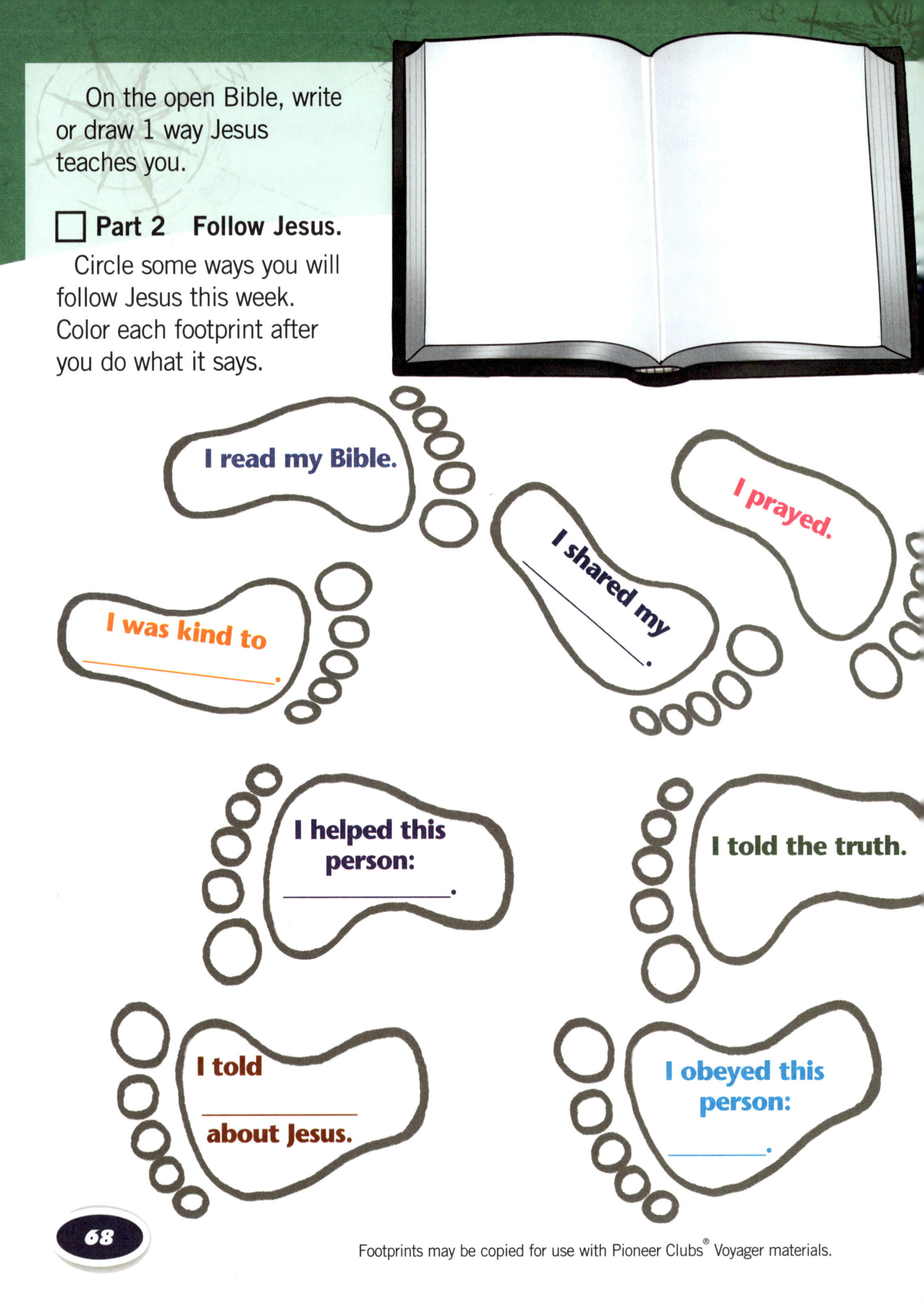

On the open Bible, write or draw 1 way Jesus teaches you.

☐ **Part 2** Follow Jesus.

Circle some ways you will follow Jesus this week. Color each footprint after you do what it says.

I read my Bible.

I shared my _____.

I prayed.

I was kind to _____.

I helped this person: _____.

I told the truth.

I told _____ about Jesus.

I obeyed this person: _____.

Footprints may be copied for use with Pioneer Clubs® Voyager materials.

4 Share the Good News

Read or listen to John 1:43-49.

☐ **Part 1   How?**
Circle a way you would use to tell people about Jesus.

Invite them to Pioneer Clubs or Sunday school. (circled)

Give a tract—a printed story about Jesus.

Tell them in person.

Write a letter.

Talk on the phone.

☐ **Part 2   What?**
Put a check in the circle by the Bible that says something you will tell.

- Jesus died for you. ✗
- Jesus wants us to talk to him. ✗
- Here's how Jesus helped me: _____
- Jesus loves you. ✗
- Jesus listens when we talk to him. ✗
- Your idea: _____

☐ **Part 3   Who?**
Think of people you can tell about Jesus: friends, family, people you meet.
Write the name or initials of someone you will tell about Jesus this week. _Dan & children_

Memory Verses   ☐ Matthew 18:14   ☐ Mark 1:17

When you learn a verse, put a Memory Verse Sticker on the back cover chart.

☐ This week I used my Bible Memory Cards to review my verses.

69

Doing What's Right
BIBLE AWARD

To earn this award, do the things listed and check off each one.

1 Following God's Rules

☐ **Part 1   Use a puppet.**

Read or listen to Leviticus 19:11. Use a puppet to tell a story of someone who breaks these rules. Tell an adult why you think God made these rules.

☐ **Part 2 Take the right paths.**

Draw lines to show the paths you will choose to follow.

sock puppet

hand puppet

Tell the truth

Tell lies

Steal from others

Respect other people's stuff

70

2 What's Most Important

☐ **Part 1   Follow Jesus.**

Read or listen to Ephesians 5:1. When you decide to follow Jesus, you decide to become more like him. Act out how you could be like Jesus in at least 1 of these situations.

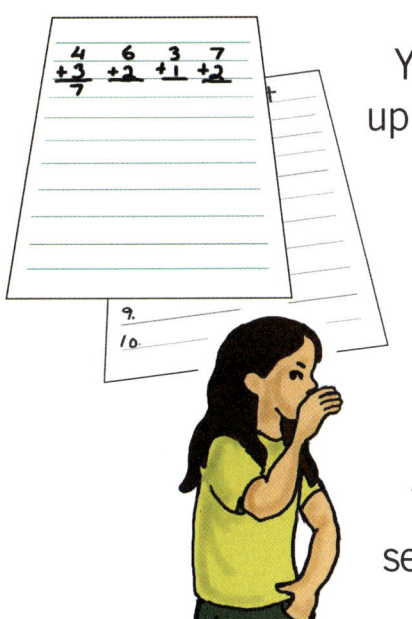

You forgot to do your homework. You think of making up an excuse to tell the teacher.

Your little brother messed up your things. You think of messing up his things.

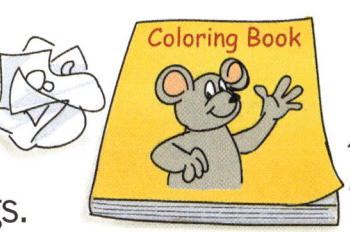

Your big sister tells you a bad secret. She says, "Don't tell!"

☐ **Part 2   Color hearts.**

How can you show Jesus that following him is important to you? Color the heart in front of what you decide to do today.

♡ I will read my Bible.

♡ I will pray.

♡ I will care about people who have needs.

♡ I will give money to God.

♡ I will obey Jesus.

♡ I will ask Jesus to help me act more like him.

3 Return Good for Evil

☐ **Part 1   Solve the problem.**

Read or listen to Leviticus 19:17-18. Talk with an adult about what this means. Help Allison make a right decision. Draw what she does.

"Allison, you're so clumsy and sloppy!"

"I saw you do that!"

Next day

Next day

What will Allison do?

• Tell how you feel. • Talk things over.
• Ask God to help.
• Tell how you feel
• Be kind. • Ask a grownup to help.

(Drawing: "It will make me nervous")

☐ **Part 2   Think of someone.**

Think of someone who sometimes is unkind to you. Tell your friends or an adult what you can say or do that would please God when that person is unkind.

4 Standing Up for What's Right

☐ **Part 1   Stand Up for God**

Moses sent 12 explorers to check out the land that God promised to the Israelites. They found out that the land had strong people living in it. 10 explorers got scared. Read or listen to what they said in Numbers 13:31. But Joshua and Caleb stood up for God. Read or listen to what they said in Numbers 13:30.

Circle an idea you will use to stand up for God when others want you to do wrong. In the box, draw how you will do that.

Ideas:

Speak up.

Remind others of the rules.

Talk to my parents or club leader.

Ask God for help.

My idea: _Tell Someone_

Tell a grown-up!

Memory Verses   ☐ Leviticus 19:11   ☐ Leviticus 19:18

When you learn a verse, put a Memory Verse Sticker on the back cover chart.

☐ This week I used my Bible Memory Cards to review my verses.

God Made Families
BIBLE AWARD

To earn thi[s]
award, do t[he]
things liste[d]
and check o[ff]
each one.

1 Learning to Obey

☐ **Part 1   Match the results.**

Read or listen to Exodus 20:12a. We are obeying God when we obey our parents. When we decide whether to obey or disobey Mom or Dad, our choice has results. Draw lines from the "no" face to what might happen if the boy disobeys. Draw lines from the "yes" face to what might happen when he obeys.

"No!"   "Yes!"

☐ **Part 2   Choose to obey.**

How will you obey your mom or dad?   Circle 1 or more ideas. Or add your own.

Try a new food   Go to bed on time.   Do a chore without complaining.   Come when called

74

2 Forgiveness Puzzle

☐ **Part 1 Do a puzzle.**

God wants us to forgive family members. But how? Solve the puzzle to find some steps you can take.

Word List

~~even~~
~~forgives~~
~~feel~~
~~anger~~
~~want~~
help

Down

1. Tell the person how you feel.
2. Don't get even.
4. Let go of anger.

Across

1. Remember God forgives you.
3. Tell the person what you want.
5. Ask God to help you.

☐ **Part 2 Take a step.**

What family member do you need to forgive? Write the first letter of the person's name here: RGSKPP

Look at the clues in Part 1. Put a check mark by the step you'll try.

3 Garlands & Chains

☐ **Part 1 Learn to be wise.**

Read or listen to Proverbs 1:8-9. Think about who God uses to make you wise. Connect these problems to the people you would ask for help.

my mother.

an aunt.

If I need to know how to put something together, I would ask…

If I'm having trouble with other kids, I would ask…

my father.

a grandparent.

If I need help with schoolwork, I would ask…

If I am feeling sad or lonely, I would ask…

an uncle.

someone else.

☐ **Part 2 Make a garland.**

Reread Proverbs 1:9. Bend pipe cleaners together. Cut out paper leaves. Tape them to the pipe cleaners. Fill in 3 leaves for your mom or dad or another adult who takes care of you. On the leaves, write what you would write in the blanks:

Thank you for teaching me _____.

I will pay attention when you teach me

_____.

Show the garland to the person you were thinking about when you made it.

4 Families Help

☐ **Part 1   Help each other.**

See how Uncle Abram helped Nephew Lot. Read or listen to Genesis 14:14-16. Cross out all Xs and Zs. Copy the other letters to find ways family members can help each other.

Give a __ __ __ __ __ __ __ __ __ __ .
cxozmplizzment

Set the __ __ __ __ __ .
zxtxablxe

(Nice shirt!)

__ __ __ __ __ each other up.
Czhexer

__ __ __ __ __ something.
Czaxrxry

Help with a __ __ __ __ __ .
chzxoxre

Come when __ __ __ __ __ __ __ .
caxxlzled

(I'm coming!)

__ __ __ __ with someone.
Pxlzazy

☐ **Part 2 Make a coupon.**

Make a coupon for a family member. Write or draw 1 way you will help the family member.

Coupon
I will help you by:

handing you tools

Love, *Jorge*

Memory Verses   ☐ Exodus 20:12a   ☐ Proverbs 1:8

When you learn a verse, put a Memory Verse Sticker on the back cover chart.

☐ This week I used my Bible Memory Cards to review my verses.

Bible Teachings
Bible Award

To earn thi[s] award, do t[he] things liste[d] and check [off] each one.

1 Praying

☐ **Part 1** "Send" a prayer to God!

Jesus told his friends—and us—how to pray. Read or listen to Matthew 6:9-13. Pretend you are mailing a prayer to God. What could you write on the envelope? What could you put inside? Connect the dots to find out.

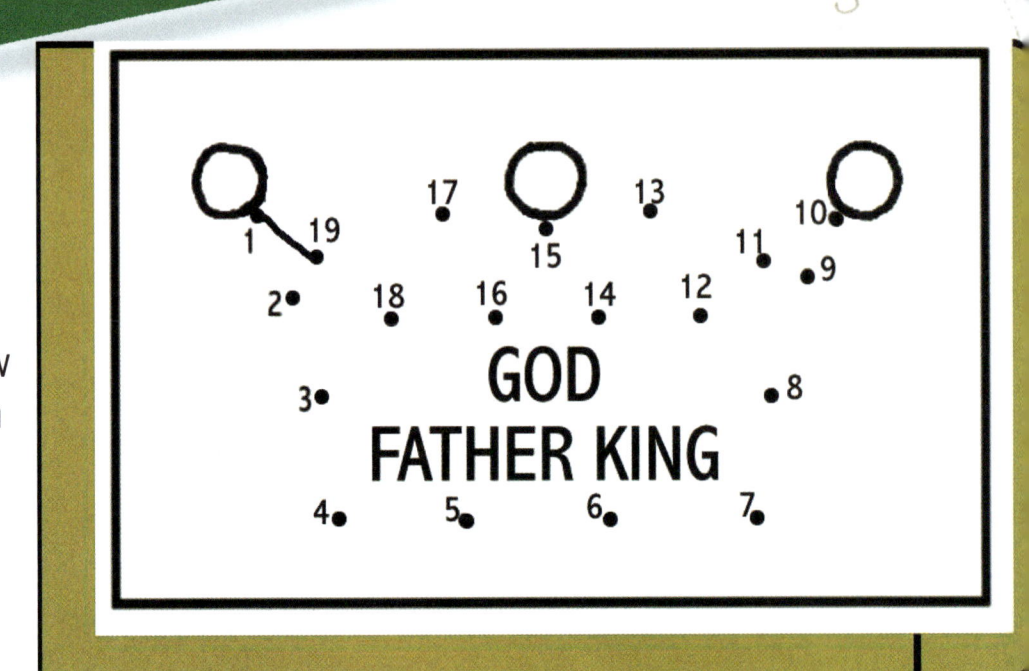

GOD FATHER KING

I want your plans to happen.

Please give me... What I need

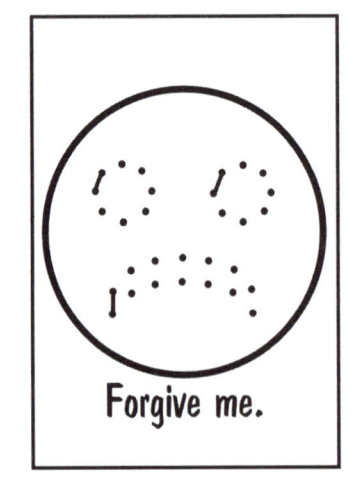

Forgive me.

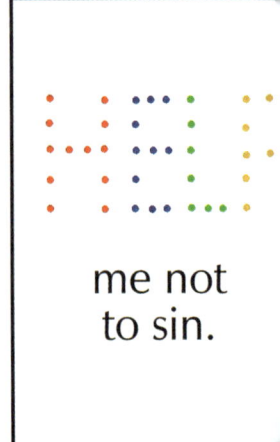

me not to sin.

☐ **Part 2** Talk to God about everything!

Look at the pictures above. Circle a way to pray from Part 1 that you will try this week.

2 Praising God

☐ **Part 1**   Finish the picture.

To praise God is to tell him how great we think he is. Read or listen to 2 Chronicles 5:13 and 6:13-14. Show how King Solomon and the people were praising God by drawing lines from the hands, harp, mouth, and horn outside to where they belong in the picture.

☐ **Part 2**   Choose a way to praise.

Choose a special way you'd like to praise God this week. You can tell him how great he is or thank him for something he has done. Draw a picture of your idea.

• sing praise songs to God • tell God thank you • play praise music •

make something beautiful for God

3 Trusting God

☐ **Part 1 Think about worries.**

Circle things you are afraid of or worried about. Or add your own idea.

my idea: _____

☐ **Part 2 Make a magnet.**

On a piece of cardboard, write, "Trust God." Add 1 of these verses that tell God's promises. God's promises can help you trust him when you're worried or afraid.

God will be with me. (Exodus 3:12)
If I admit I've done wrong, God will forgive me. (1 John 1:9)
God's love lasts forever. (Psalm 118:1).
The Lord is my shepherd. (Psalm 23:1)

Put a piece of sticky magnet on the back.

4 Listening to Jesus

☐ **Part 1 Match ways to listen to Jesus.**

Saul was an angry man who put Christians in prison! He had studied God's Word, but he wasn't listening to Jesus. Read or listen to Acts 9:3-8, 17. Draw lines to match the ways Jesus spoke to Saul and the ways we listen to Jesus today.

☐ **Part 2
See how to listen to Jesus.**

Look at the 2 cartoons. Talk to a grownup about these questions:
1. What do you think is happening?
2. How is each kid listening to Jesus?
3. What do you think Jesus told the kid?
4. What did the kid do to obey Jesus?

☐ **Part 3   Listen to Jesus.**

Has Jesus been trying to speak to you? Color the top traffic light *red* if you think Jesus wants you to *stop* doing something bad this week. Color the bottom one *green* if he wants you to *go* do something good. Color the middle one *yellow* if you will *wait* and see what you hear from Jesus this week.

Memory Verses   ☐ Matthew 6:9   ☐ Exodus 3:12a

When you learn a verse, put a Memory Verse Sticker on the back cover chart.

☐ This week I used my Bible Memory Cards to review my verses.

Artist
Activity Award

To earn this award, do the things listed and check off each one:
- [ ] 1. Draw or Paint
- [ ] 2. 3-D Art
- [ ] 3. Clay Modeling
- [ ] 4. God's Art
- [ ] Extra Credit

1 Draw or Paint (do 2)

☐ Silly Circles

You will need:
- paper
- pencil
- markers
- ruler
- different-sized round lids and cups

Use a ruler and pencil to make some lines across your paper. Now trace around different-sized lids and cups onto the paper. Draw your circles on and between the lines. Color in some parts of your design.

☐ Crackle Painting

You will need:
- white paper or newsprint
- crayons
- black paint
- water
- container for paint
- paintbrushes

Use crayons to draw a picture or design. Press hard to get lots of wax on the paper. Now crumple your paper carefully. Don't tear it! Spread it out flat again.

Add water to black paint, about twice as much water as paint. Paint over your picture. This will make your drawing look as though someone made it many years ago.

☐ **Sponge Art**

You will need:
- paper
- sponges
- scissors
- paints
- pie pans
- water

Dip a sponge in water and squeeze it dry. Cut it into a fun shape. Make more shapes if you like. Pour paint into pie pans. Touch a sponge to the paint. Press it on paper. Press it more times, harder and more gently. Print a couple of times without adding more paint. Now use your shapes to make a finished design.

☐ **Chalk Lines**

You will need:
- pine board
- nail
- string
- chalk
- construction paper
- hairspray
- hammer

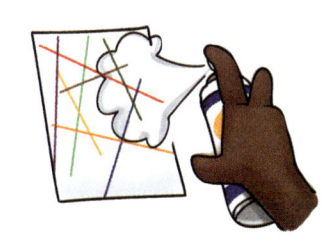

Have an adult tie a piece of string to a nail hammered partway into a large board. Coat the string with chalk dust by rubbing the chalk along it. Put paper on the wood. Pull the string tight with 1 hand. Hold the end on the edge of the paper. Snap the string onto the paper with the other hand.

Add more chalk to the string. Turn the paper and snap the string on a different place. Keep adding chalk lines until you have a design you like.

Have an adult spray hairspray on your design to keep it from smudging.

☐ **Sidewalk Chalk Art**

Get permission to draw chalk pictures on a sidewalk or parking lot.

☐ **Your Choice:** _____

2 3-D Art (do 1)

☐ Lots of Shapes

You will need:
- construction paper
- cardboard
- glue stick
- scissors
- optional: glitter glue, sequins

Cut strips of construction paper in different widths and lengths. Make circles, squares, triangles, and "springs" out of them. Glue your shapes on a piece of cardboard in any design you want. If you have them, add glitter or sequins.

☐ Sunflower

You will need:
- paper plate
- brown and yellow paint
- construction paper
- scissors
- unshelled sunflower seeds
- paintbrushes
- glue

Paint the plate yellow. Paint a brown circle in the center of the plate. Put dots of glue on sunflower seeds. Glue them onto the brown area.

Cut a stem out of green construction paper. Glue it onto another sheet of construction paper. Glue on the paper plate flower at the top of the stem. Cut out leaves. Roll them around your finger so that they curl a little. Glue them on the stem.

☐ Your Choice: _____

3 Clay Modeling (do 1)

☐ Fancy Sand Castle

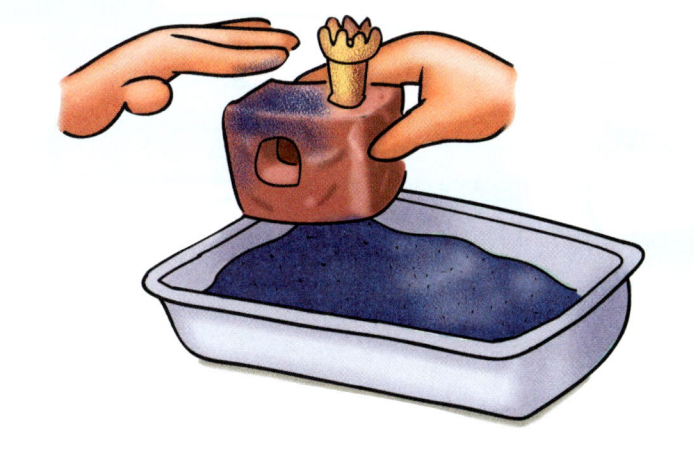

You will need:
- nontoxic self-hardening clay
- plastic knives
- sand
- powdered tempera paint
- glitter
- large bowls or bins

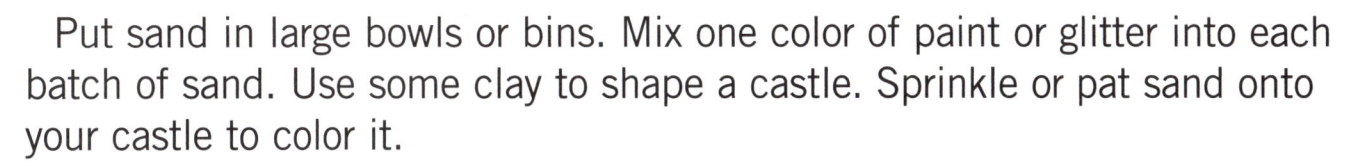

Put sand in large bowls or bins. Mix one color of paint or glitter into each batch of sand. Use some clay to shape a castle. Sprinkle or pat sand onto your castle to color it.

☐ Useful Stuff Holder

You will need:
- nontoxic self-hardening clay
- construction paper
- scissors
- table knife
- rolling pin
- ruler

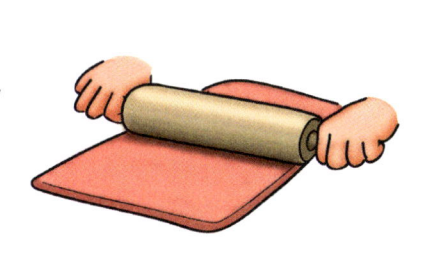

Cut out a construction paper rectangle, 3 by 15 inches (7.5 by 38 cm). Roll out some clay. Press the rectangle onto it. Cut around the rectangle. Press the two short ends of the clay rectangle together to make a tube. Roll out more clay. Set your clay tube on the rolled-out clay. Cut around it as shown. Press the edges of the new piece of clay onto the end of the tube. You may press more clay shapes onto the holder to decorate it.

☐ Your Choice: _____

4 God's Art

☐ **Think about rainbows.**

Read Ezekiel 1:28. Ezekiel is comparing the glory of God to how a rainbow looks. Circle some words that describe what you think of rainbows, a form of God's art. Draw your own rainbow here.

colorful   boring   awesome   GREAT

huge   blah   so-so

beautiful

Extra Credit (do 1)

☐ Give 1 of your art projects to someone as a gift.

☐ Visit a museum, art store, or artist's studio.

Bible Times ACTIVITY AWARD

To earn this award, do the things listed and check off each one:
- [ ] 1. Pretend to live in Bible times.
- [ ] 2. Dress the part.
- [ ] 3. Do daily chores.
- [ ] 4. Learn a job.
- [ ] 5. Make Bible-times food.
- [ ] 6. Listen to a Jesus story.
- [ ] Extra Credit

1 Pretend to live in Bible times.

- [ ] **Think about what your home might be like.**

Finish the dot-to-dot puzzles to see what your home might have been like.

your sleeping mat

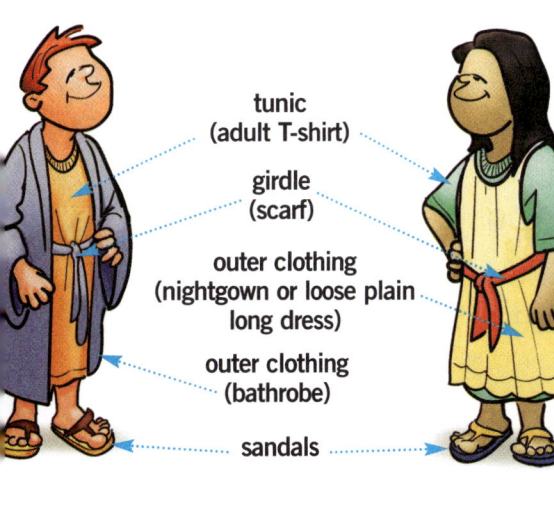

- tunic (adult T-shirt)
- girdle (scarf)
- outer clothing (nightgown or loose plain long dress)
- outer clothing (bathrobe)
- sandals

2 Dress the part. (do both)

- [ ] **Get Bible-times clothes.**

Boys and girls in Bible times wore very different clothes from what you wear. Use these modern clothes to imitate Bible-times sandals, tunics, sashes, and robes.

☐ **Have a dress-up relay.**

People in Bible times slept on mats on the floor. For this game, each team gets a big towel as a pretend mat. All players wear their Bible-times clothing.

Players pretend go to sleep and then get up in the morning. The first runners run to the mat, take off sandals and outer clothing, lie down, and close their eyes. Then they get up, dress, and run back to tag the next runners.

3 Do daily chores. (do both)

☐ **Herd the sheep.**

IT is a shepherd. The other players are the sheep. Pick a place to be the sheep pen. Whenever IT tags a "sheep," that player has to follow IT to the pen. The last sheep penned is the next IT.

☐ **Carry the firewood.**

Roll and tape sections of newspaper to make 10 "logs" for each team.

Have a relay race. Put paper logs in a pile for each team. The first runner brings back the whole pile and hands it off to the second runner. The second runner puts all the logs back on the pile and then runs back to tag the next person, who picks up the logs again. If your group is small, play as one team. Time yourselves.

4 Learn a job. (do 1)

Children learned how to do jobs from an older person, often a parent, in Bible times.

☐ **Potter**

You will need:

- clay
- string

To make a model of an oil lamp from Bible times, make a clay bowl. Pinch one side for a spout. Curl up some string. Put it in your lamp. Let one end hang out of the spout. *Important:* Do not add oil or light your wick. Your lamp is only for fun. It is not safe to use.

☐ **Woodworker**

chair

table

You will need:
- board
- saw
- hammer
- nail
- sandpaper

bed

door

Have an adult help you saw through a board. Sand the edges smooth. Hammer a nail into the piece you cut off.

Jesus learned woodworking from his earthly father, Joseph. Circle what you think Jesus might have learned to make.

storage chest

window

☐ **Your Choice:** _____

5 Make Bible-times food. (do 1)

Always have an adult help you when you are cooking.

☐ **Fruit Kabob with Yogurt**

You will need:
- 1-inch (25 mm) pieces of apple, melon, pineapple
- ½ cup (125 ml) plain yogurt
- 2 tablespoons (30 ml) honey
- wooden skewer
- bowl
- large spoon
- measuring cup and spoons

Thread fruit on a skewer. Mix yogurt and honey in a bowl. Dip your fruit in it.

☐ **Microwave Millet**

You will need:

- 1 cup (250 ml) millet
- salt
- measuring cup
- mesh strainer
- 2 cups (500 ml) water
- microwave-safe container, cover
- spoon
- optional: butter, honey, or grated cheese

Wash and drain the millet. Combine millet, water, and a pinch of salt. Cover loosely and microwave 20 minutes on high. Let sit for 5 minutes. Eat plain or with butter, honey, or cheese.

☐ **Lentil Soup**

You will need:

- can of lentil soup
- spoon
- pot or microwave-safe container
- can opener

Pour the soup in the pot. Heat over medium heat. Stir to keep soup from sticking to the pan and burning. Eat pita bread with the soup.

6 Listen to a Jesus story.

☐ **Pretend to go hear Jesus.**

Pack some food. Pretend to walk for a long way to go where Jesus is. What do you think the Bible-times people would have seen and heard around them?

Have an adult tell you a story that Jesus told, such as Luke 15:11-24 or Luke 15:3-10. Listen to what Jesus said. Share your food with the people around you.

Extra Credit (do 1)

☐ Learn to knead bread.

☐ Put on a "living history" demonstration for an audience. Act as if you are really someone from Bible times. Explain the things you are doing.

Let's Pretend
Activity Award

To earn this award, do the things listed and check off each one:
- ☐ 1. Acting Games
- ☐ 2. Animal Acting
- ☐ 3. Create Your Own Skit
- ☐ 4. Imitate God
- ☐ Extra Credit

Acting Games (do 2)

☐ **Simon Says**

Play regular *Simon Says.* But IT asks players to act like something. *Ideas:*

- robot
- kangaroo
- astronaut floating in space
- trees blowing in the wind
- fish swimming

☐ **Move to the Music**

Play music. IT calls out different ways to move to the music. *Ideas:*

- glide
- hop
- twist
- run
- slouch along
- walk proudly

☐ **Noisy Circle**

Sit in a circle. One person makes a noise. The next person copies it and adds a new noise. The third person copies the new noise and makes another. Keep going around the circle. *Option:* Have each person try to repeat all the noises in order as new noises are added.

baa

baa click

click tweet

tweet bang

☐ **Your Choice:** _____

2 Animal Acting (do both)

☐ **Animal Noises**

Pretend to be these animals. Show how you would move and what noises you would make.

    cat being chased by a dog

    dog chasing a squirrel

    prairie dog too big for a friend's hole

    bear with a hurt paw

    hungry dog asking for food

    thirsty elephant smelling water

    your idea: _____

☐ **Owner and Pet**

Find a partner. Think of a pet. You may choose a normal pet like a dog or a silly pet like a hippo. Pretend to be the owner. Have your partner pretend to be the pet. Act out:

    feeding the pet   teaching the pet a trick

    giving the pet exercise   your idea:

_____

Now switch. You be the pet and your partner be the owner. Do the same pet or another.

3 Create your own skit. (do both)

☐ **Write a skit.**

Make up a story about 1 of these things. Keep it short. Have someone write it down. Be sure to have as many people or animals as you have friends to act in it.

You and your friends find buried treasure while hiking.
Your family goes to a toy store to buy a birthday present for a friend.
A dog gets loose on the field when you and your friends are playing a sport.
Your idea: _____

☐ **Act out your story.**

Make a copy of your story for each friend. Each friend takes 1 of the parts. Practice your parts. Act out your story together.

4 Imitate God

☐ **Read Ephesians 5:1-2a.**

When we put on a skit, we imitate—or act like—someone else. Who should we act like in real life?

_____

Extra Credit (do 1)

☐ Put on your skit for another club or your parents.
☐ Go see a play.

Making Music
ACTIVITY AWARD

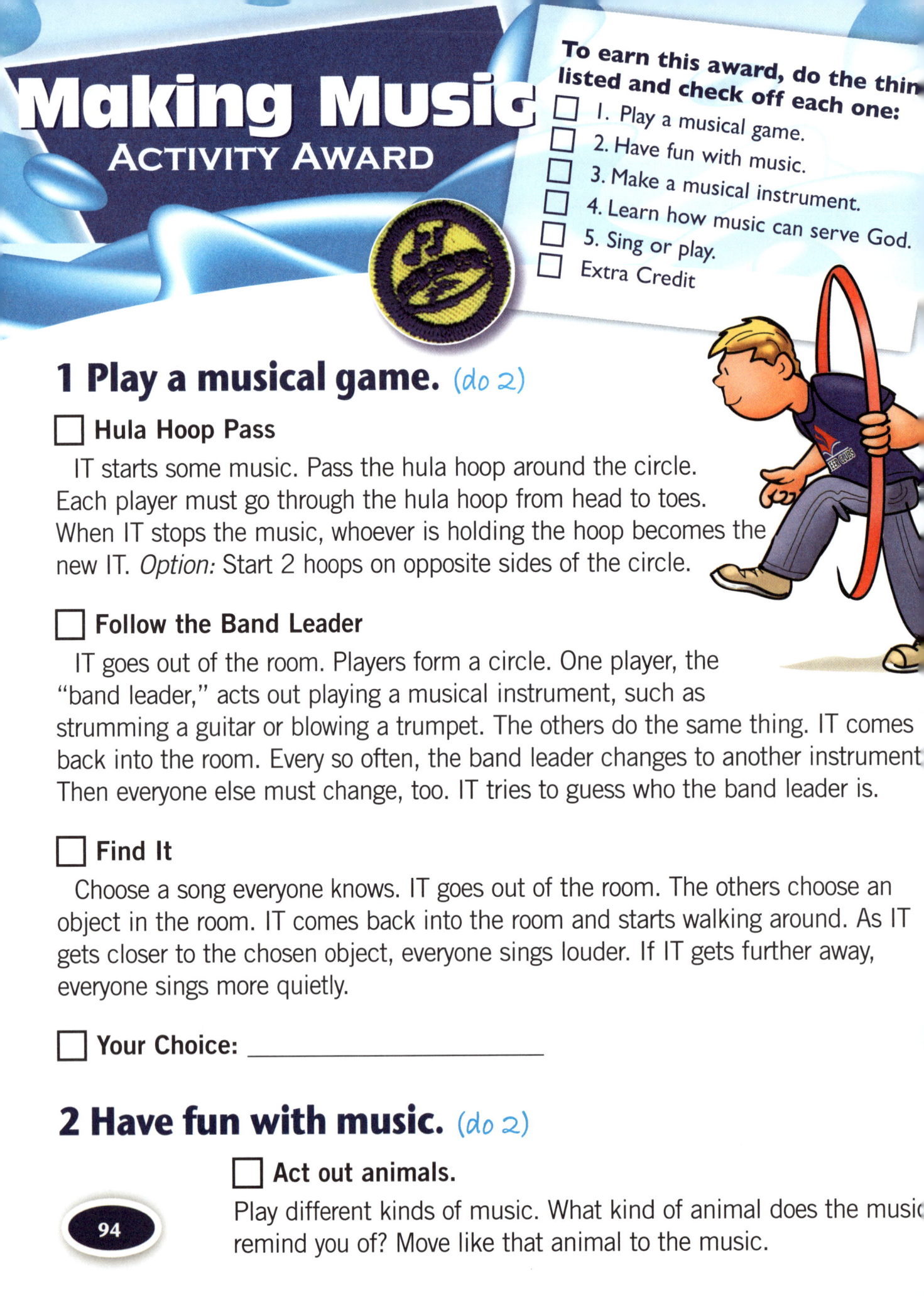

To earn this award, do the things listed and check off each one:
- [ ] 1. Play a musical game.
- [ ] 2. Have fun with music.
- [ ] 3. Make a musical instrument.
- [ ] 4. Learn how music can serve God.
- [ ] 5. Sing or play.
- [ ] Extra Credit

1 Play a musical game. (do 2)

- [ ] **Hula Hoop Pass**

   IT starts some music. Pass the hula hoop around the circle. Each player must go through the hula hoop from head to toes. When IT stops the music, whoever is holding the hoop becomes the new IT. *Option:* Start 2 hoops on opposite sides of the circle.

- [ ] **Follow the Band Leader**

   IT goes out of the room. Players form a circle. One player, the "band leader," acts out playing a musical instrument, such as strumming a guitar or blowing a trumpet. The others do the same thing. IT comes back into the room. Every so often, the band leader changes to another instrument. Then everyone else must change, too. IT tries to guess who the band leader is.

- [ ] **Find It**

   Choose a song everyone knows. IT goes out of the room. The others choose an object in the room. IT comes back into the room and starts walking around. As IT gets closer to the chosen object, everyone sings louder. If IT gets further away, everyone sings more quietly.

- [ ] **Your Choice:** _____

2 Have fun with music. (do 2)

- [ ] **Act out animals.**

   Play different kinds of music. What kind of animal does the music remind you of? Move like that animal to the music.

☐ **Wave streamers.**

Cut lengths of colorful ribbon or crepe paper streamers. Tie them together at 1 end. Play music. Move around, waving your streamers to the music.

☐ **Play rhythms.**

Find some friends. Each person needs 2 pencils to tap together. Tap the pencils in a slow, even rhythm. Tap twice as fast. Now have some tap slow and the rest tap twice as fast—at the same time.

Choose a conductor to conduct a "song" made up of taps. The conductor points to each group in turn to play their rhythm or to both groups to play at the same time.

Other rhythm ideas:

loud tap, soft tap, soft tap, loud tap, soft tap, soft tap
tap, tap, pause, tap, tap, pause

☐ Your choice: _____

3 Make an instrument. (do 1)

☐ **Drum**

You will need:

- balloon
- construction paper
- markers
- rubber bands
  (or painters or electrical tape)
- snack chip can
- scissors
- glue or tape

Cut construction paper to fit around the can. Decorate the construction paper. Glue or tape it around the can. Blow up a balloon to stretch it. Let the air out. Cut the neck off the balloon.

Ask someone to hold the can still. Stretch the top of the balloon over the open end of the can. You may need a partner to help you. Rubber-band or tape the balloon in place.

Play your drum, using pencils for drumsticks.

☐ **Tambourine**

You will need:

- 2 heavy-duty paper plates
- chenille wires (pipe cleaners)
- hole punch
- jingle bells
- markers

Decorate the bottoms of the 2 plates with markers. Hold the 2 plates together, facing each other. Punch holes through both rims. Use the chenille wires to lace the plates together. String jingle bells on the chenille wires as you lace.

☐ **Horn**

You will need:

- paper towel tube
- scissors
- strong tape
- paper cup
- aluminum foil

Cut open the paper towel tube. Make it skinnier, about 1 inch (25 mm) wide. Tape all the way around the tube in at least 2 places. Poke a hole in the bottom of a paper cup. Make the hole just big enough to stick the tube in it. Stick the tube only a little way into the cup. Tape it on. Cover your whole horn with foil.

☐ **Your Choice:** _____

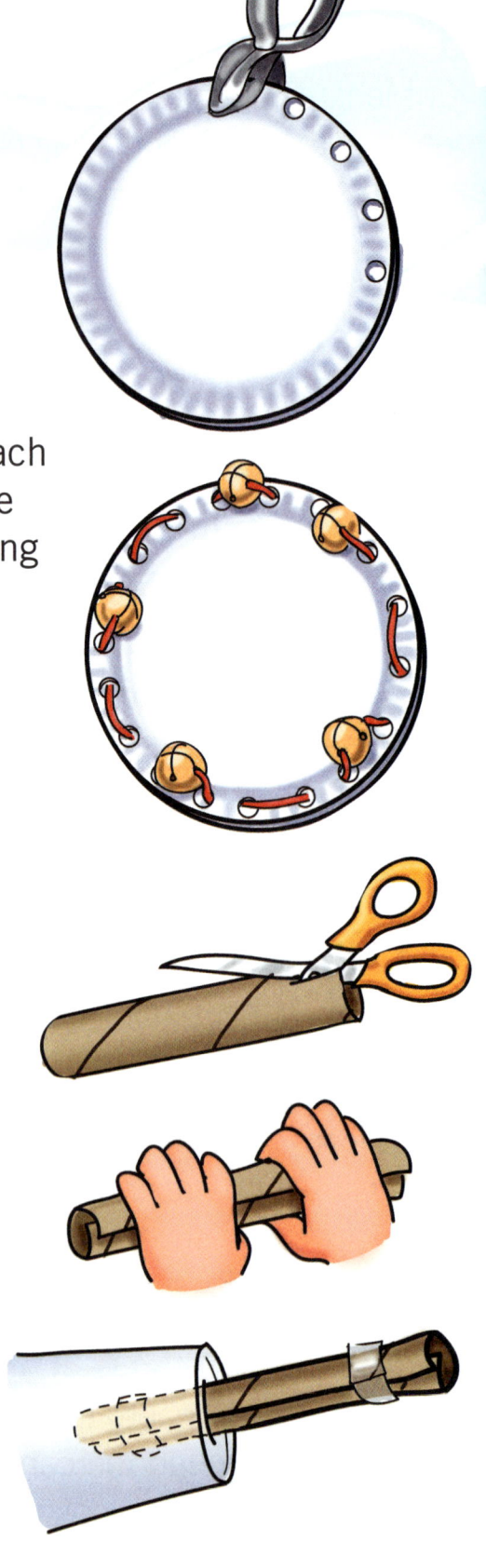

4 Learn how music can serve God.

☐ **Read Psalm 150:1, 3, 5.**

Who should we praise with music? _____
Look at the pictures of instruments in the verses. Circle 1 your homemade instrument is like.

5 Sing or play. (do 2)

☐ **Sing songs in club.**

Learn the Pioneer Clubs theme song. Learn a praise song. Take turns suggesting other songs to sing. *Option:* Play your instrument while you sing.

cymbals

harp

trumpet

none of them

☐ **Make up a praise song.**

Make up your own praise words to a song you know. *Option:* Play your instrument while you sing it.

☐ **Play along.**

Play along with the radio or a recording on your instrument.

☐ **Your choice:** _____

Extra Credit

☐ Try a real musical instrument that you have never played before.

Story Fun
ACTIVITY AWARD

To earn this award, do the things listed and check off each one:
- ☐ 1. Read or listen to a story.
- ☐ 2. Write a story.
- ☐ 3. Listen to a Bible story.
- ☐ Extra Credit

1 Read or listen to a story.

☐ **Enjoy a story.**

Write the name of the story here: _____

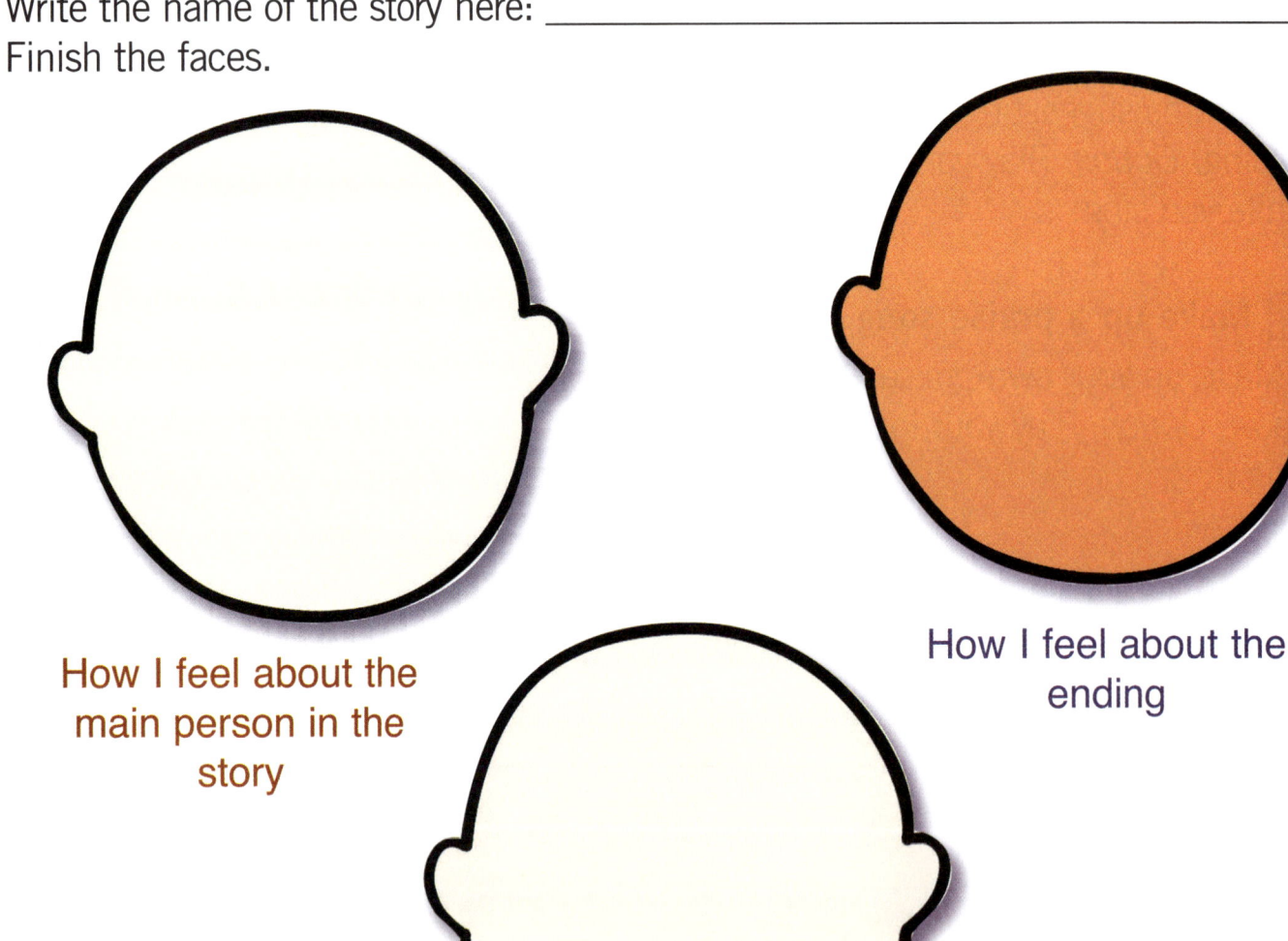

Finish the faces.

How I feel about the main person in the story

How I feel about the ending

How much I like the story

2 Write a story. (do 2)

☐ **Change the ending.**

Make up a new ending to a story you know. Write it down, draw a picture, or tell someone your new ending.

☐ **Make up a story.**

Find a picture you like. Make up a story to go with it. Draw a picture of what happens. Tell someone the story in your own words. Show your picture.

☐ **Make a picture book.**

Make at least 4 pages in your book. Draw a picture on each page. Write a sentence about each picture.

Story ideas:

The Talking Frog

The Flying Bicycle

The Bad Bad Hair Day

A Day at the Zoo

Six Little Kittens

Your Idea: _____

☐ **Make a story from cut-out words.**

Copy this page and cut out these words. Or cut words out of a newspaper. Use them to tell a story. Draw a picture if you like.

a mad cat scared the dog ran under over

the		
the	went	scared
a	ran	log
a	jumped	dog
on	felt	cat
at	looked	store
over	was	boy
under	thought	girl
to	mad	friend
for	sad	dad
about	glad	mom

Page may be copied for use with Pioneer Clubs® Voyager materials.

☐ **Your choice:** _____

3 Listen to a Bible story.

☐ **Learn about God.**

Use the Bible or a Bible story book. Read or listen to a story. Check off the 1 you do:

_____ God Calls to Samuel
(1 Samuel 3:1-10)

_____ Daniel and the Lion's Den
(Daniel 6:1-28)

_____ Jesus Brings Lazarus Back to Life
(John 11:1-6, 17-44)

_____ My Choice: _____

Extra Credit (do 1)

☐ Read or tell a story to a younger child.

☐ Talk to someone whose job is writing. What does this person like about writing?

☐ Visit a library. Ask a librarian to help you find the kinds of stories you like.

101

Clothes
ACTIVITY AWARD

To earn this award, do the things listed and check off each one:
- [ ] 1. Clothes Care
- [ ] 2. Clothes that Match
- [ ] 3. Clothes for My Life
- [ ] 4. Clothes for Weather
- [ ] 5. Clothing from Isaiah 61:10
- [ ] Extra Credit

1 Clothes Care (do 3)

Ask an adult to teach you these skills.

- [ ] **Learn to fold and hang shirts.**

Learn which kinds of shirts should be folded and which kinds should be hung.

Play *Duck, Duck, Goose* with shirts. Put hangers in the middle of the circle. IT carries several shirts, some that should hang and some that should be folded. When IT drops a shirt in a player's lap, the player must hang it or fold it before IT can run around the circle and back to the player.

- [ ] **Fold pairs of socks.**

Have a relay race. Put a pair of socks for each player in a pile for each team. Players run to the pile, fold a pair of socks, and run back to tag the next player.

- [ ] **Sort a pile of laundry.**

Sort light colors from dark colors. Keep thin, fragile clothes in a different group than sturdy clothes like jeans.

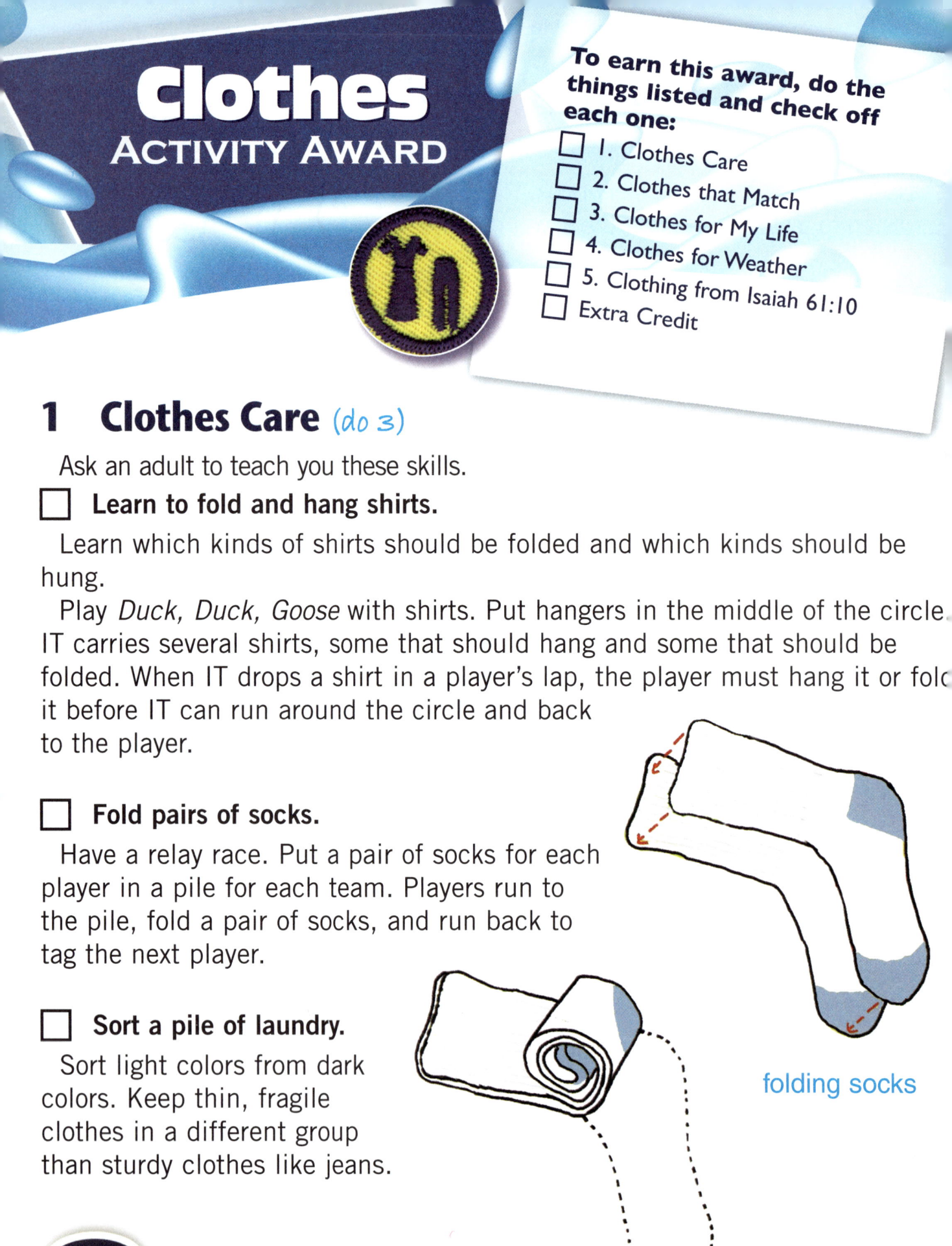

folding socks

☐ **Wash out a stain.**

Rub some dirt on an old shirt to make a stain. Spray the dirt with stain remover. Scrub it with a toothbrush. Rinse it in cool water. Hang it up to dry.

☐ **Wash or polish a pair of shoes.**

☐ **Your choice:** _____

2 Clothes that Match

☐ **Make a *Concentration* game.**

Cut out lots of shirts and pants or skirts from catalogs and magazines. Find items with different colors and patterns. Find dressy and casual items. Make sure each piece of clothing has another piece that goes together well with it. See the pictures for examples.

Glue each picture on a separate index card. On the other side of each card, write T if the picture is of a top and B if the picture is of a bottom. Mix up the cards. Put them face-down in rows.

The first player turns up 1 T card and 1 B card. If the player thinks those 2 pieces of clothing go together well, he or she says, "Match!" and keeps the cards. If not, he or she says why they don't go together. Then the player puts those cards back. Take turns choosing cards.

3 Clothes for My Life

☐ **Draw.**

Draw what you wear to play in the summer. Draw what you wear to play outside in rainy or snowy weather. Draw what you wear to church or school.

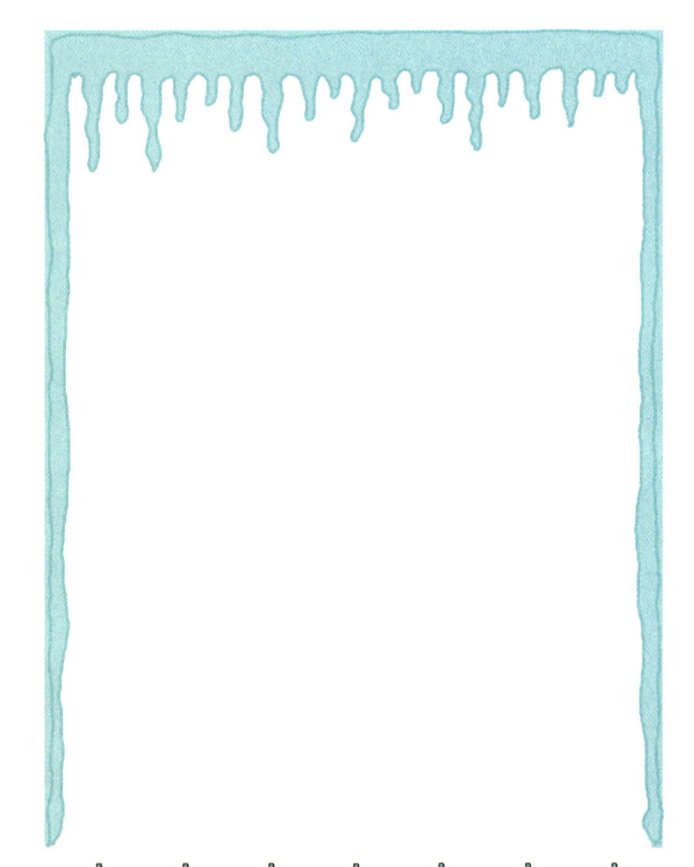

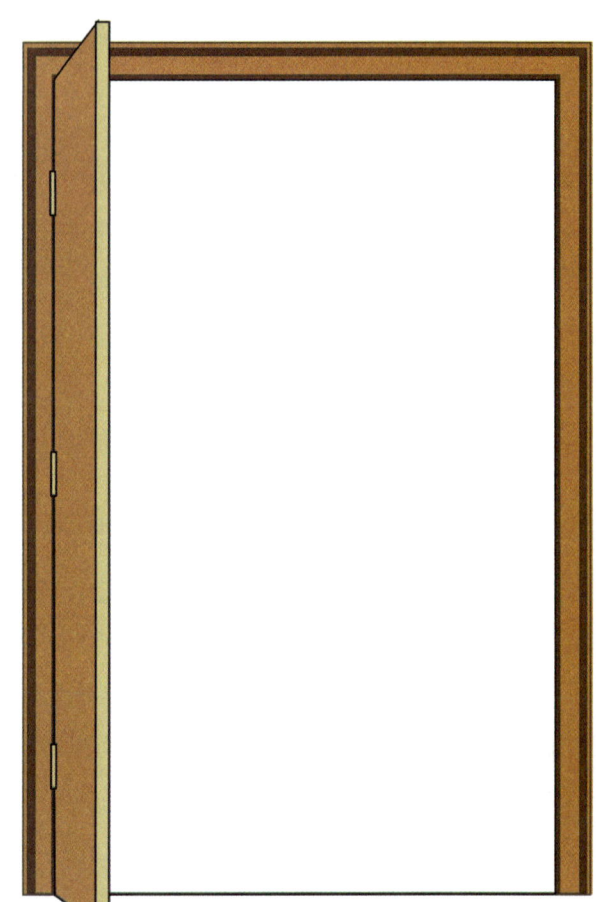

4 Clothes for Weather

☐ **Play a game.**

Collect lots of adult-size clothes for sunny, rainy, and cold weather. Put them in a pile.

Form 2 teams. Choose 1 player to be IT. IT calls out 1 type of weather: "Sunny," "Rainy," or "Cold." The first 2 players run to the pile and find something that fits that kind of weather. They put it on fast. Whoever is the fastest gets to be IT next.

5 Clothing from Isaiah 61:10

☐ **Talk it over.**

Talk with an adult about how you can wear an idea like salvation or goodness. Then draw what you would look like wearing these if they were real pieces of clothing. *Ideas:*

Salvation

Goodness

Extra Credit

☐ Talk to someone who wears special clothing, like a uniform, for his or her job. Find out what the clothing does.

Club Helper
ACTIVITY AWARD

To earn this award, do the things listed and check off each one:

☐ 1. Invite friends to club.
☐ 2. Help your club.
☐ 3. Make "Welcome" tags.
☐ 4. Make up a song.
☐ 5. Thank your club leader.
☐ 6. Read or listen to John 9:4.
☐ Extra Credit

1   Invite friends to club.

☐ **Make invitations.**

You will need:
- construction paper
- scissors
- glue
- markers
- optional: copies of this page

Cut a sheet of construction paper in half. Fold each half to make a card. Glue a copy of the invitation on this page to the inside of each card. Fill in the blanks. Or write all the information. Think of 2 friends you'd like to invite to club. Put a name on each card. If you like, make invitations for more friends. Give cards to your friends this week.

Pioneer Clubs meets on

_____ at _____.
(day)   (place)

We start at _____.
                    (time)

It's really fun! We play games, do cool activities, and learn about God. Would you like to come with me?

_____
(your name)

Invitation may be reproduced for use with Pioneer Clubs® Voyager materials.

2 Help your club.

Choose 3 ways to help your club. Do all 3 at the next 3 club meetings. Put a star in a circle for 1 of your choices each time you help that way.

WEEK	1	2	3
Alyssa			
Brad			
Chris			
Daniela			
Jamie			

Hand out supplies.

Mark who is at club.

Help clean up.

Help set up chairs.

Do another job: _____

107

3 Make "Welcome" tags.

☐ **Prepare for visitors.**

You will need:
- large self-stick tags
- markers

Decorate "Welcome" tags to give to club visitors.

4 Make up a song.

☐ **Help visitors feel welcome.**

Make up a song or rap that your club can sing or say when a new kid comes to visit. Use a familiar tune such as "Old MacDonald" or "Row, Row, Row Your Boat." Include ideas like these:

We're happy to have you!
Welcome to club!
Come back soon!

5 Thank your club leader. (do 1)

Now that you have helped in club, you know there is a lot of work to do. Choose 1 way to tell your club leader "thank you."

☐ **Sign a photo.**

Write your name on the front. On the back, write 1 thing you like best about Pioneer Clubs.

☐ **Make a card.**

Include 1 or 2 things that you like best about Pioneer Clubs.

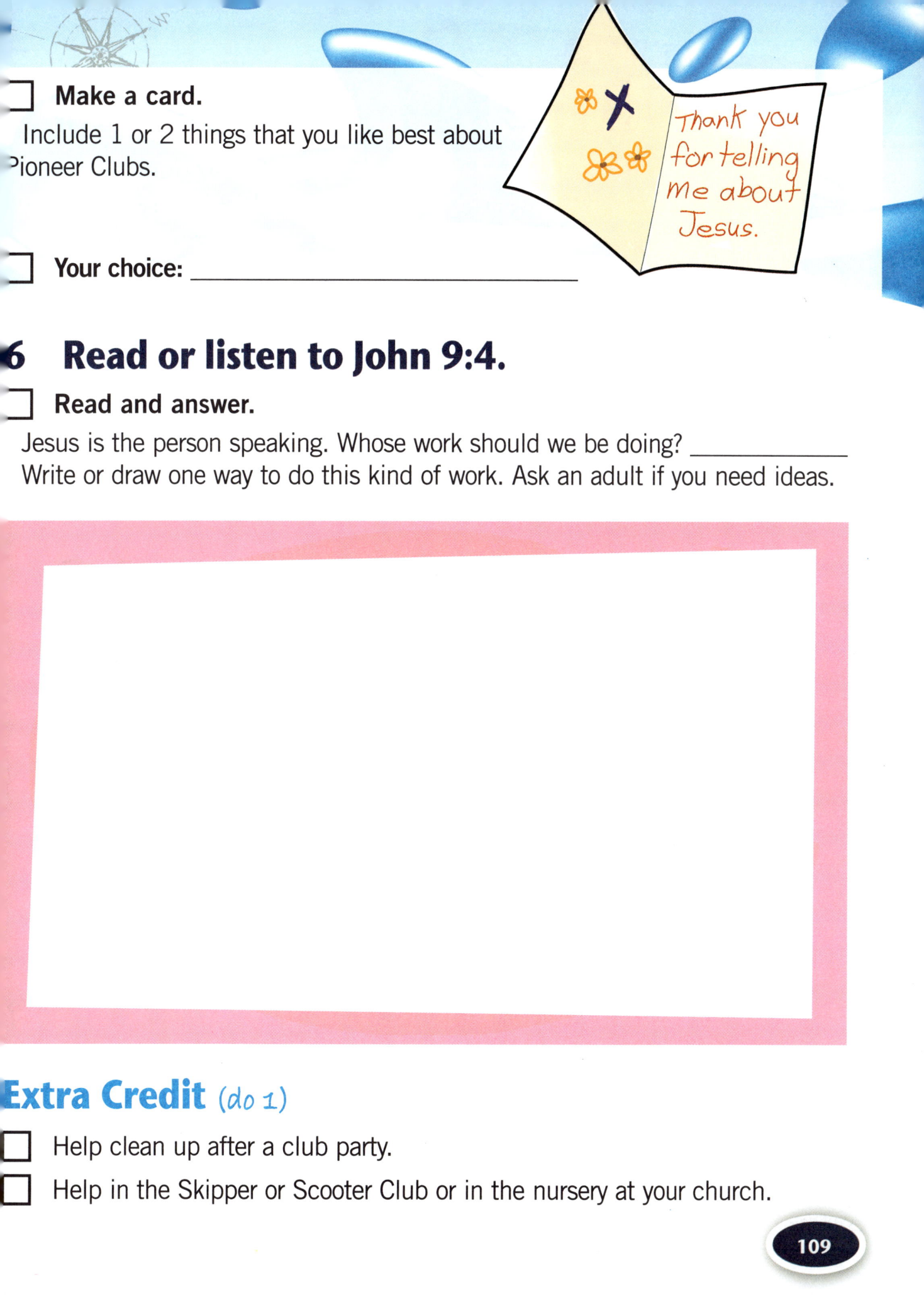

☐ **Your choice:** _____

6 Read or listen to John 9:4.

☐ **Read and answer.**

Jesus is the person speaking. Whose work should we be doing? _____
Write or draw one way to do this kind of work. Ask an adult if you need ideas.

Extra Credit (do 1)

☐ Help clean up after a club party.

☐ Help in the Skipper or Scooter Club or in the nursery at your church.

Cooking
ACTIVITY AWARD

To earn this award, do the things listed and check off each one:
- [ ] 1. Learn safety rules.
- [ ] 2. Practice measuring.
- [ ] 3. Make recipes.
- [ ] 4. Thank God.

1 Learn safety rules.

- [ ] **Match the pictures.**

The first rule of cooking is to always have a grownup help you. Match the pictures to the blanks to learn some other rules.

Wash your _____ before starting.

Wash uncooked _____ .

Don't _____ your fingers while cooking.

Don't eat anything with raw _____ in it.

Use _____ when moving pans into or out of an oven.

2 Practice measuring. (do both)

☐ **Measure dry things.**

Use flour, sugar, or sand. Use the back of a knife to smooth off the extra amount in the cup or spoon. Measure these amounts:
　___ 1 teaspoon (5 ml)
　___ ½ cup (125 ml)

☐ **Measure liquids.**

Learn how the side of a liquid measuring cup is marked. Measure these amounts of water. Pour the water into a bowl using the cup's spout.
　___ 1 cup (250 ml)
　___ ½ cup (125 ml)

3 Make recipes. (do 3)

☐ **Ladybug Apple**

You will need:
- red apple
- raisins
- cream cheese (whipped or softened)
- 2 toothpicks
- knife

Have an adult help you slice the apple in half and scoop out the core.

Dip raisins in cream cheese. Stick them to the back of the apple for ladybug spots. Stick a raisin onto each toothpick. Stick the toothpicks into the apple for antennae.

☐ **Tuna Salad**

You will need:

- easy-open can or bag of tuna
- 1 tablespoon (15 ml) pickle relish or chopped celery
- 2 to 3 tablespoons (30 to 45 ml) mayonnaise
- crackers
- bowl
- spoon
- measuring spoons

Have an adult help you open the can and drain the tuna. Mix tuna and mayonnaise in a bowl. Mix in pickle relish or celery. Spread on crackers. Makes about a dozen crackers.

☐ **Cookies**

Use slice-and-bake cookie dough. Have an adult turn on the oven and read the package for how to make the cookies. Slice the dough. Grease the cookie sheet if you need to. Put the sliced dough on the cookie sheet. Set a timer when you put the sheet in the oven.
Take out cookies when done. Let cool and eat!

☐ **Painted Bread**

You will need:

- food coloring
- milk
- bowls
- new paintbrushes
- white bread
- toaster
- smock or old shirt

Wear a smock or old shirt to protect your clothes. Pour milk in bowls. Mix a little food coloring in each. Have a paintbrush for each bowl. Paint designs on your bread. Toast your bread lightly. Eat it, or use it to make a sandwich.

☐ **Pizza Breadsticks**

You will need:
- package of breadstick dough, 8 sticks
- pizza sauce
- cookie sheet
- nonstick cooking spray
- bowl
- optional: can opener

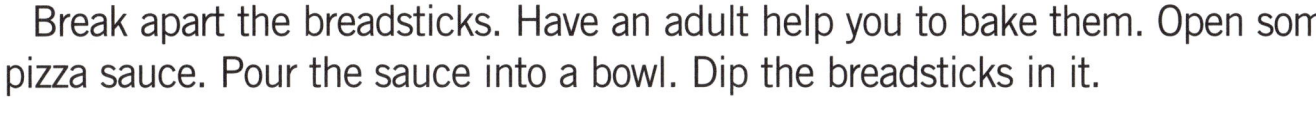

Break apart the breadsticks. Have an adult help you to bake them. Open some pizza sauce. Pour the sauce into a bowl. Dip the breadsticks in it.

☐ **Your Choice:** _____

4 Thank God.

☐ **Read or listen to Exodus 16:2, 3, 11-15, 31.**

God did miracles to give the Israelites food. He gives you food, too. Draw a picture of your favorite food. Learn one of these table prayers or another one so you can tell God "thank you" when you eat.

*God is great, and God is good,
And we thank him for our food;
By his hand we all are fed;
Give us, Lord, our daily bread.*

*Come, Lord Jesus, be our Guest,
And let your gifts to us be blessed.*

*For food and all your gifts of love,
We give you thanks and praise.
Look down, O Jesus, from above,
And bless us all our days.*

Family Fun
ACTIVITY AWARD

To earn this award, do the things listed and check off each one:

☐ 1. Have fun with your family.
☐ 2. Plan a family party.
☐ 3. Picture your family.
☐ 4. Treat your family special.
☐ 5. Learn about God's family.
☐ Extra Credit

1 Have fun with your family.

☐ **Circle the things you like to do with your family.**

Put a star by the activities you'd like to try. Draw in your own ideas. Act out the ones you choose. Ask your family to do one of these things with you.

114

2 Plan a family party. (do both)

☐ **Make plans.**
If you could have a party just for your family, what would you want to do? Choose a theme. Write or draw some ideas in the chart.

Party Theme	Snacks & Drinks	Decorations	Activities & Games
Birthday			
Holiday			
My idea: _____			

☐ **Make a snack bag.**

Decorate a paper bag for your family. Put some snacks in it to get them in the mood for a family party.

3   Picture your family. (do 1)

☐ **Magnetic Picture Frame**

You will need:

- construction paper
- markers
- scissors
- tape
- pictures of family members that you can cut
- adhesive magnet strips

Draw a design that has places for your pictures. You could draw a house or plane with lots of windows. Cut out a hole big enough for each picture. Or trim your pictures to fit the openings.

On the back of your design, tape the pictures into the places you cut out. Attach a magnet strip to the back of your design.

☐ **Family Photo Album**

You will need:

- camera
- photo album or scrapbook

Take pictures of your family. Put them in a photo album or scrapbook. Write or tell about each picture.

116

4   Treat your family special.

☐ **Choose special things to do.**

Match each person in your family with one special thing you will do for him or her this week.

Mom	say something nice
	give a hug
Dad	offer to help with a project
	make a favorite snack
Brother(s)	do one of his or her chores
	call on the phone to say, "I love you"
Sister(s)	put a kind note under a pillow
	your idea: _____
Others	

Make a coupon for each family member. Draw something on each coupon that reminds you of what you decided to do for him or her. Give the coupons to your family members. They can give them back to you when they want you to do that nice thing for them.

5   Learn about God's family.

☐ **Read or listen to John 1:12.**

Talk with an adult about how to become a member of God's family.

Extra Credit

☐ Create a family newspaper. Ask each person in your family to write, type, or draw things about your family. Show your leader a copy of your newspaper.

Family Helper
ACTIVITY AWARD

To earn this award, do the things listed and check off each one:

☐ 1. Learn inside chores.
☐ 2. Learn outside chores.
☐ 3. I will help.
☐ 4. Be a happy helper.
☐ Extra Credit

1 Learn inside chores. (do both)

☐ **Practice inside chores.**

Circle the chores that you do in your home. Learn 2 new chores. Put check marks by them.

☐ **Run a chores race.**

Pick a chore such as folding towels, matching socks, or another chore of your choice. For a relay race, each runner could fold one towel from a pile or match one pair of socks from a basket. Or play against yourself—have someone time you and see if you can beat your own record.

2 Learn outside chores.

☐ **Practice outside chores.**

Circle outside chores you already do or know how to do. Put a check mark by chores you could do outside.

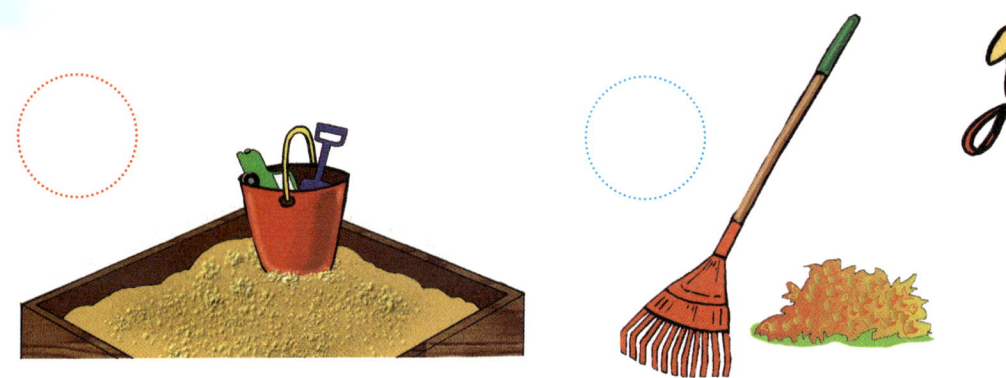

Practice a new outside chore with your club group or a family member.

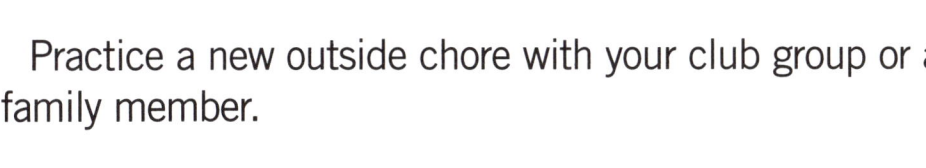

I learned to _____.

3   I will help.

☐ **Use this chart.**
Fill in chores you do. For one week, mark the chart as you do each job.

Family Helper Chart

Sunday					
Monday					
Tuesday					
Wednesday					
Thursday					
Friday					
Saturday					

Have a parent sign this Family Helper certificate.

Family Helper certificate

_____ has learned to be a good helper.

Signed: _____
Parent

Chart and certificate may be copied for use with Pioneer Clubs® Voyager material.

4 Be a happy helper.

☐ **Learn what God says.**

Draw a face in the first circle to show how you feel about doing chores.

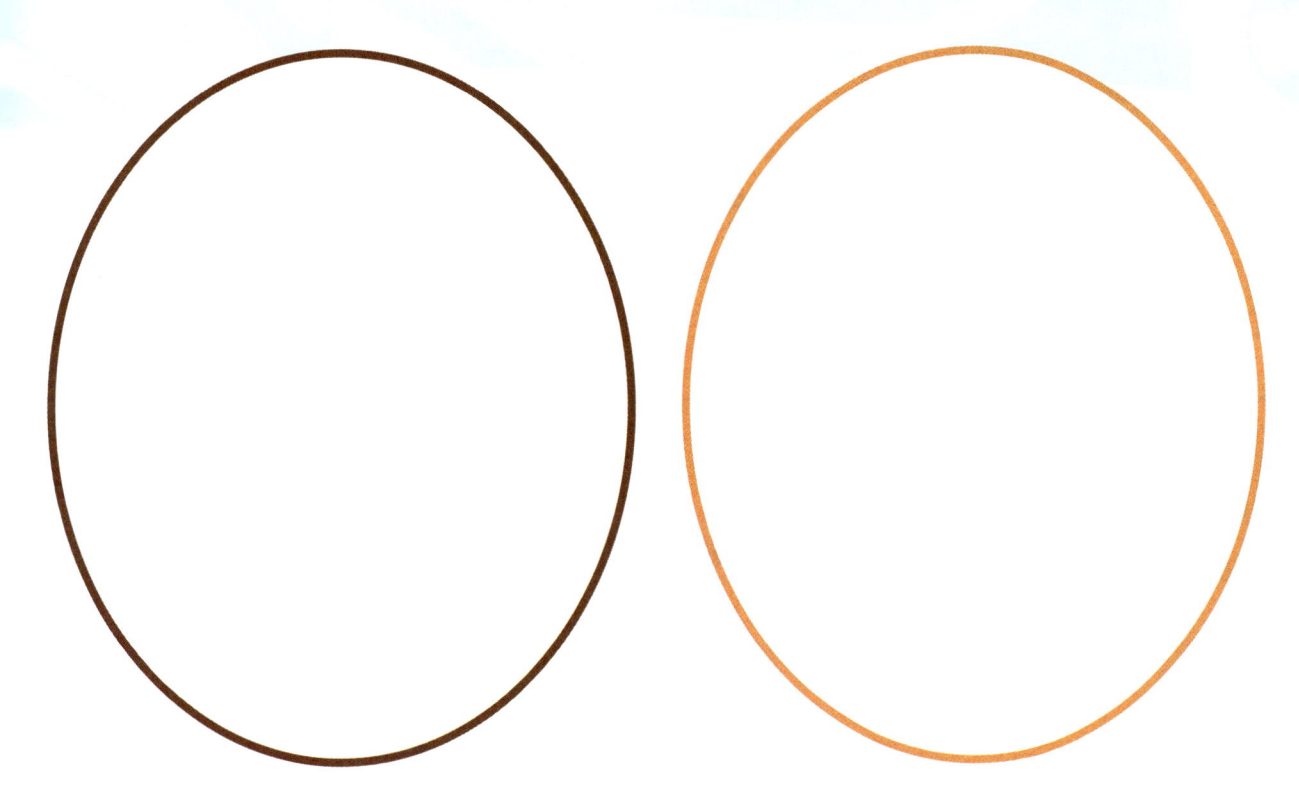

Now read or listen to Philippians 2:14-15a. Draw another face that shows how these verses say you should do your work. Why are you supposed to do chores this way? Check any correct answers.

__ Because complaining makes you feel better.
__ Because God wants you to do the right thing.
__ Because arguing might get you out of it.

Talk with an adult about what could help you feel better about doing chores. Memorize Philippians 2:14. Ask God to help you do your chores the way the Bible says.

Extra Credit (do 1)

☐ Help someone in your family with a project.

☐ Help someone in your family clean a room.

Feeling Good
Activity Award

To earn this award, do the things listed and check off each one:
- ☐ 1. Good Looks
- ☐ 2. Good Food
- ☐ 3. Good Moves
- ☐ 4. Good Rest
- ☐ 5. God's Goodness
- ☐ Extra Credit

1 Good Looks (do all)

To look your best and feel your best, you need to take good care of your body.

☐ **Learn to brush your teeth.**

You will need:
- sink
- toothbrush
- toothpaste
- mirror

Have a parent or club leader show you the correct way to brush your teeth. Try it, and get an adult to check you. Look in the mirror when you are brushing to be sure you are doing it right. Talk about when you should brush your teeth.

☐ **Learn to care for your hair.**

You will need:
- comb or brush
- mirror

Comb or brush your hair. Look in the mirror to see if it looks nice. Talk with a parent or club leader about how and when to wash your hair.

! Never share your comb or brush with anyone.

122

☐ **Learn to wash your hands.**

You will need:
- sink
- soap
- towel

Wet your hands and get them soapy. Don't run the water while you lather soap on. Clean under your fingernails. Clean palms and backs. Wash long enough—sing "Twinkle, Twinkle, Little Star" once before you rinse and dry your hands.

2 Good Food (do both)

☐ **Learn which foods are good.**

Circle the foods that are good for you. Check with an adult. Put an X through the foods you should not eat much of.

☐ **Make a good snack.**

Plan a snack that's good for you. Use ideas from the foods you circled. Think about which foods might taste good together.

My snack idea is: _____.

3 Good Moves (do 1)

☐ **Make up an exercise routine.**

Put together a 15-minute set of exercises that you could use every day. *Ideas:*
- toe touches
- jumping jacks
- sit-ups
- push-ups
- jump rope
- running in place

Be sure to do some stretches to warm up first. Think about putting your routine to music.

Check off each day that you do this routine.

Sunday	Monday	Tuesday	Wednesday	Thursday	Friday	Saturday

☐ **Go for a walk.**

Take a 15-minute walk outdoors or indoors. Take an adult with you if you walk outdoors.

4 Good Rest (do both)

☐ **How much is enough sleep?**

Between the ages of 6 and 9, you should get about 10 hours of sleep each night. Mark what time you need to get up in the mornings on the Get Up clock. Figure out what time you should go to bed to get 10 hours of sleep. Fill in the Go to Bed clock.

GO TO BED   **GET UP**

☐ **Have a bedtime relay race with friends.**

Make 2 piles of items you would use to get ready for bed. *Ideas:* Toothbrushes, pajamas, washcloths, bedtime reading, clocks. Have 1 item for each runner.

Run a relay race. Each runner runs to that team's pile, picks up 1 thing, and runs to tag the next runner.

5 God's Goodness

☐ **Read or listen to Psalm 139:14.**

Draw a picture here showing how you feel about the way God made you.

Extra Credit

☐ Do 1 of the following for 20 minutes: ride a bike, skate, swim, play soccer or basketball, run, or jog.

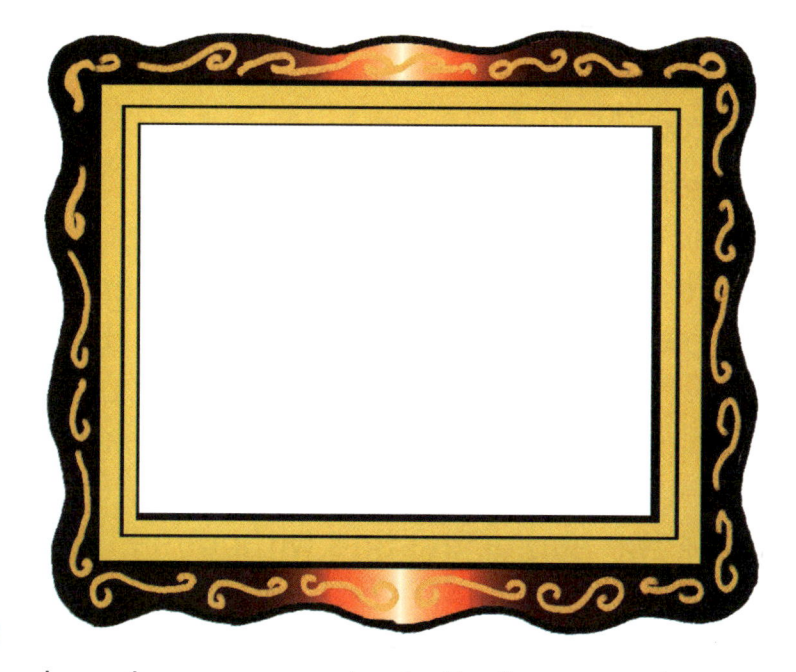

International Fun
Activity Award

To earn this award, do the things listed and check off each one:
- ☐ 1. Play new games.
- ☐ 2. Eat a new food.
- ☐ 3. Make something fun.
- ☐ 4. Learn about a new culture.

1 Play new games. (do 2)

Play some games children play in other cultures.

☐ Lion's Cub (Africa)

This game uses a small toy lion (or other fierce animal, such as a tiger or bear). The "lion" sits with his or her back to the other players, about 10 feet (3 m) away. The lion places the toy lion behind his or her back. Players take turns trying to sneak up and steal the toy lion. But the lion can roar and turn around to try and catch the thief. If the thief gets caught before grabbing the toy lion, the lion gets another turn. If a player does steal the toy lion, he or she is the next lion.

☐ Hagoo (Native Alaskan)

Two teams line up facing each other. A player from each team stands, at the opposite end of the line from each other. They bow to each other and call out, "Hagoo," which means "Come here." The 2 players walk toward each other, looking at each other's face. The other players in the lines try to make the walkers smile or laugh.

Players in the lines may not reach out or touch the walkers. A player who walks to the end of the line without smiling or laughing rejoins the same team. If a walker smiles or laughs, he or she joins the opposite team. Then the next 2 players have a turn.

☐ **Lost a Couple (Pakistan)**

All players except IT stand in a circle in pairs. Be sure to remember who your partner is. One person in each pair steps forward. The other steps back. Now there should be 2 circles, 1 on the outside, and 1 on the inside. The inside circle begins walking to the right and the outside circle walks left. IT calls out, "Stop." Players must find their partner, grab hands, and sit down before IT counts to 10.

☐ Your Choice: _____

2 Eat a new food. (do 1)

Try a food from a different part of the world.

☐ **Tropical Fruit Treats (South Asia)**

You will need:
- orange
- banana
- shredded coconut
- small plate
- saucer or wide, shallow bowl
- knife

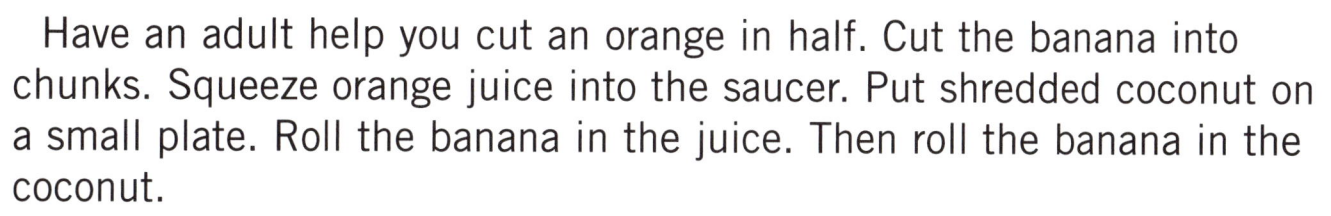

Have an adult help you cut an orange in half. Cut the banana into chunks. Squeeze orange juice into the saucer. Put shredded coconut on a small plate. Roll the banana in the juice. Then roll the banana in the coconut.
Serves 1-2.

! Have an adult help whenever you cut or heat food.
Use oven mitts when moving things into or out of a hot oven.

☐ **Mooncakes (China)**

You will need:
- ¼ cup (60 ml) sugar
- 1 egg yolk
- ½ cup butter (125 ml), at room temperature
- 1 cup (250 ml) flour
- 1 cup (250 ml) strawberry jam or Chinese red bean paste
- large bowl and spoon
- plastic wrap
- cookie sheet
- oven mitts

Have an adult help. Preheat the oven to 375° F (190° C). Mix butter, sugar, and egg yolk in a large bowl. Then mix in the flour. Form the dough into a large ball. Wrap it in plastic wrap. Chill for half an hour.

Roll pieces of dough into small balls. Put the balls on a cookie sheet. Make a dent in each ball with your thumb. Fill it with jam. Bake the mooncakes for about 20 minutes, until slightly browned. Let the cakes cool before eating. Makes 24.

☐ **Fresh Veggie Pizza (Mediterranean)**

You will need:
- 1 ready-made pizza crust (or pita bread)
- 8-ounce (250 g) package cream cheese, at room temperature
- 1 cup (250 ml) sour cream
- 1 envelope powdered ranch dressing mix
- 2 cups (500 ml) raw vegetables (such as carrots, mild peppers, tomatoes, cauliflower, cucumbers), cut into small pieces
- mixing bowl and spoon

If you need to bake the pizza crust, get adult help. (Or use pita bread.) Stir together the cream cheese, sour cream, and dressing mix. Spread it on the crust. Top with the raw vegetables.

☐ **Your Choice:** _____

3 Make something fun. (do 1)

☐ **Origami Hat (Japan)**

1. Fold a half sheet of newspaper in half, matching the short sides together.

2. Fold down each corner of the folded side to make a triangle shape.

3. Fold up the bottom edge on one side, to hold the triangle folds in place.

4. Flip the hat over. Fold up the bottom edge on the other side.

5. Open the hat to wear it.

☐ **Drum (Africa)**

You will need:
- 2 drinking cups (paper or plastic)
- masking tape
- shoe polish
- old rags
- permanent markers

Tape the 2 cups together, bottom to bottom. Use long pieces of masking tape to completely cover the cups' sides and open tops. Cover with shoe polish and let it dry. Use markers to decorate the drum with patterns and designs.

Tap the drum with your fingers to play it.

☐ **Christmas Cracker (England)**

You will need:
- toilet paper tube
- tissue paper
- ribbon
- scissors
- stickers or old Christmas wrapping paper
- small candies, toys, confetti
- glue

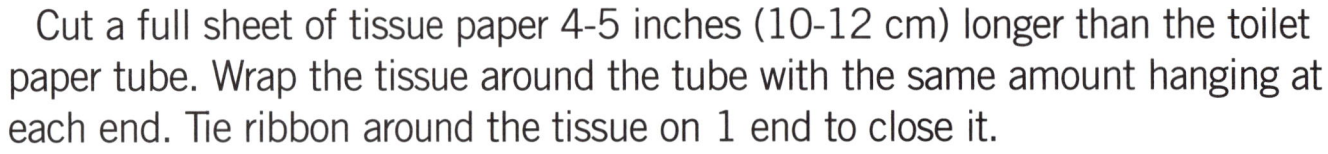

Cut a full sheet of tissue paper 4-5 inches (10-12 cm) longer than the toilet paper tube. Wrap the tissue around the tube with the same amount hanging at each end. Tie ribbon around the tissue on 1 end to close it.

Fill with candies, tiny toys, and confetti. Make your own confetti using a hole punch and colored paper, if you like. Close with another piece of ribbon. Decorate with stickers, Christmas paper, or drawings.

In England, "crackers" are given at parties. Hold both ends of the cracker and pull sharply. One end will "crack" open and the goodies will spill out.

☐ Your Choice: _____

4 Learn about a new culture.

☐ **Read a story or watch a video.**

Your club leader or parent can help you find a story or video that will help you learn about another culture. Ask him or her to read or watch with you.
The story or video is named:

_____

Something in it that I thought was very interesting:

Manners
Activity Award

To earn this award, do the things listed and check off each one:
- [ ] 1. Practice good manners.
- [ ] 2. Be polite to others.
- [ ] 3. Use good manners at home.
- [ ] 4. Practice table manners.
- [ ] Extra Credit

Practice good manners. (do both)

☐ **Circle the correct words.**

What do you say?

You want a turn.	please	thank you
You get a gift.	please	thank you
Your friend lets you use a toy.	please	thank you
You would like more to drink.	please	thank you

Role play some other times you could use "please" and "thank you."

☐ **Make thank-you cards.**

You will need:
- construction paper
- markers
- stickers, ribbons, or other decorations
- scissors
- glue

Make some thank-you cards. Decorate them with markers or by gluing things on. Leave room inside to write a note. Send one when you get a gift or someone does something nice for you.

2 Be polite to others. (do 1)

☐ **Practice being polite.**

Show how you would act for at least 2 of these:
- You see someone drop something.
- You let someone else go first.
- You see someone carrying lots of things.
- You open a door for someone.
- Your idea: _____.

☐ **Make a poster about being polite.**

You will need:
- posterboard or heavy paper
- pictures you have cut out
- markers
- glue

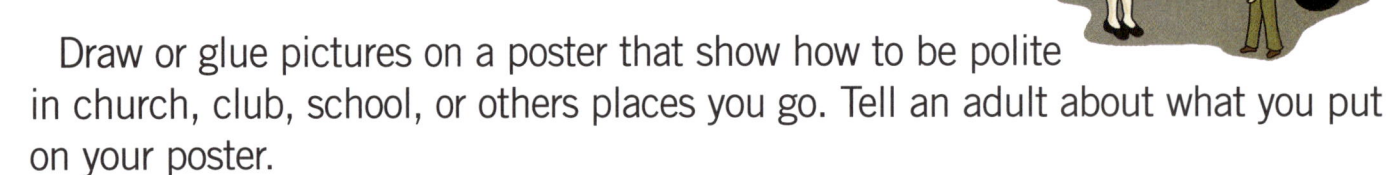

Draw or glue pictures on a poster that show how to be polite in church, club, school, or others places you go. Tell an adult about what you put on your poster.

3 Use good manners at home. (do both)

☐ **Phone Manners**

Make a game to play with someone. Copy the cards here and on the next page. Put them upside down in a pile. Pass a phone from player to player. Whoever gets the phone takes a card. He or she uses the phone to show what to say in that situation. Have an adult help you know what to say. Remember to speak clearly and politely.

You find out that you dialed a wrong number.	An adult calls and wants to speak to your father, who is busy.
A boy wants to talk to your older sister.	A caller wants to talk to your mother, who is not home.

Cards may be copied for use with Pioneer Clubs® Voyager materials.

You call your aunt to say "thank you" for a gift.	You call to invite a friend to your place to play.
You call your parent and ask if you may stay at your friend's place for dinner.	A kid calls and asks for someone you've never heard of.

Cards may be copied for use with Pioneer Clubs® Voyager materials.

☐ Answering the Door

Pretend you are at home. Someone comes to your door. Act out what you would say or do.
- A neighbor wants to see your parent.
- Your friend wants you to play.
- Your brother's or sister's friend comes over to study.
- You see a person you don't know.
- Your idea: _____.

4 Practice table manners. (do all)

☐ Table Setting

Draw the napkin, fork, knife, and spoon where they belong on the placemat. Then try setting a real table.

☐ **Good-Looking Table**

Have someone show you simple ways to fold a napkin.

☐ **Table Rules**

Color the right way to do each thing.

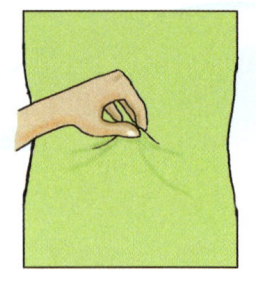

Scarf Fold

Extra Credit

☐ Practice good manners at a real or pretend meal in club or during a real meal at home. Help set the table and be polite during the meal. Tell your club leader what you did.

Missions
Activity Award

To earn this award, do the things listed and check off each one:

- ☐ 1. Learn about missions.
- ☐ 2. Pray for missions.
- ☐ 3. Make a missions mobile.
- ☐ 4. God says, "Go!"
- ☐ 5. Play games from other countries.
- ☐ Extra Credit

1 Learn about missions.

☐ **Find a story about missionaries.**

Ask your club leader, church librarian, or parents to help you find a missions story. You may read or listen to a book or watch a video.

Circle which you did.

2 Pray for missions. (do 1)

☐ **Make a prayer chain.**

You will need:
- construction paper
- scissors
- tape or glue

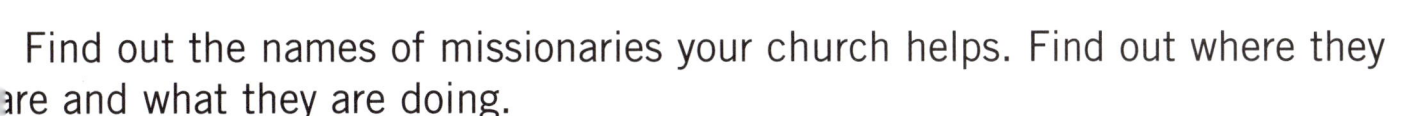

Find out the names of missionaries your church helps. Find out where they are and what they are doing.

Cut the paper into strips. On each strip, write the name of a missionary, a country your missionaries live in, or a missions prayer request. Tape or glue the ends of the first strip to make a loop. Connect the other loops to form a chain. Hang the prayer chain in your club room or home to remind yourself to pray for the missionaries and their work.

☐ **Animal prayer reminders.**

Gather stuffed or bean bag animals from other parts of the world. *Ideas:* A panda for China, a kangaroo for Australia, a zebra for Africa. Pray for the country or area where each of the animals lives.

☐ **Your Choice:** _____

3   Make a missions mobile.

☐ **Make a mobile to remember missionaries.**

You will need:
- 4 plastic drinking straws
- tape
- 4 pictures of missionaries your church supports
- scissors
- glue
- construction paper
- thread

Tape 2 straws together end to end to form a long straw. Do the same with the other 2 straws. Tape the 2 long straws together to form an X. Cut 4 shapes out of construction paper. Make them big enough to glue the pictures on.

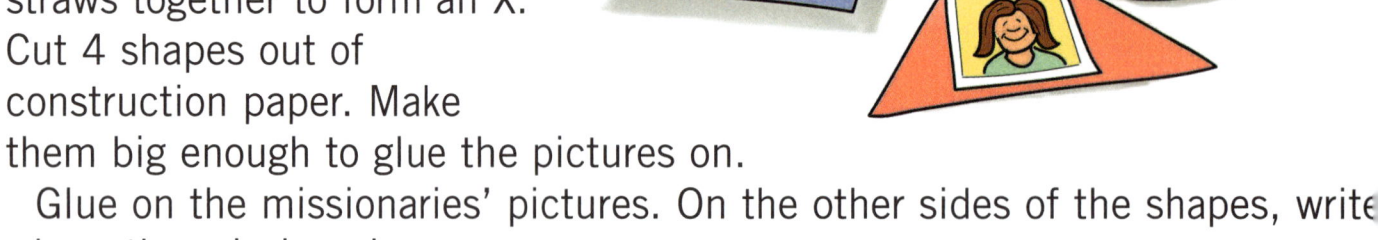

Glue on the missionaries' pictures. On the other sides of the shapes, write where the missionaries serve.

Tape 1 end of a thread to the top of each shape. Tape or tie the other end to 1 end of a straw. Use enough thread so the pictures hang down. Tie thread around the center of the X to hang your mobile.

4 God says, "Go!"

☐ **Read or listen to Matthew 28:19a.**
What does God say is the job of a missionary? Circle 1.

> Teach people in your town to play tag.
>
> Pray for people in all countries.
>
> Help people everywhere learn about and believe in Jesus.

5 Play games from other countries. (do 2)

☐ **Chopsticks Relay (China)**

You will need:
- pair of chopsticks for each team
- napkins or paper towels
- wastebasket for each team

Divide into equal teams. Wad up the napkins or paper towels into balls, 1 for each player. The first player on each team picks up a paper ball with the chopsticks, runs to the wastebasket for that team, and drops the ball in. Then the player runs back, giving the chopsticks to the next player.

☐ **Laughing Hyenas (Africa)**

Players sit or stand in a circle with IT in the middle. When IT says, "Laugh," everyone begins laughing. When IT says, "Stop," everyone must stop laughing instantly. Anyone who can't stop becomes the new IT.

☐ **Grab the Beret (France)**

You will need:
- beret or other type of hat

Divide into 2 teams. Teams line up facing each other at opposite ends of the room.

Each team counts off, so everyone has a number. Start the numbering on opposite ends of the 2 lines.

Put the hat in the middle of the floor. IT calls out a number. The 2 players who have that number try to snatch the hat and run back to their team without being tagged by the other team's player. The chasing player becomes the next IT if the player who grabbed the hat is not tagged. If the person with the hat is tagged, he or she is the next IT.

☐ **Your Choice:** _____

Extra Credit

☐ E-mail a child in a missionary family. Tell him or her about what you do with your family, in club, and at school. Ask about the kid's life and for prayer requests.

My Friends
Activity Award

To earn this award, do the things listed and check off each one:
- [ ] 1. Play a friends game.
- [ ] 2. Do things with friends.
- [ ] 3. Meet a new friend.
- [ ] 4. Make a snack to share.
- [ ] 5. Be a friend.
- [ ] Extra Credit

1 Play a friends game.

☐ **Game**

Each player should mark 10 blank index cards for this game:

Color Card—color 2 cards your favorite color

Food Card—on 2 cards, draw a common food that's one of your favorites

Animal Card—on 2 cards, draw a common animal that's one of your favorites

Sister Card—on 2 cards, write how many sisters you have

Brother Card—on 2 cards, write how many brothers you have

Each player keeps 1 set of his or her cards. Mix up all the extra cards and put them in a pile, backside up. This is your "Friend Pile." Form a circle around the Friend Pile. Hold your 5 cards so no one else can see. When it's your turn, choose a player. Ask if he or she has a card that matches 1 of yours. *Example:* "Chris, do you have 2 brothers?"

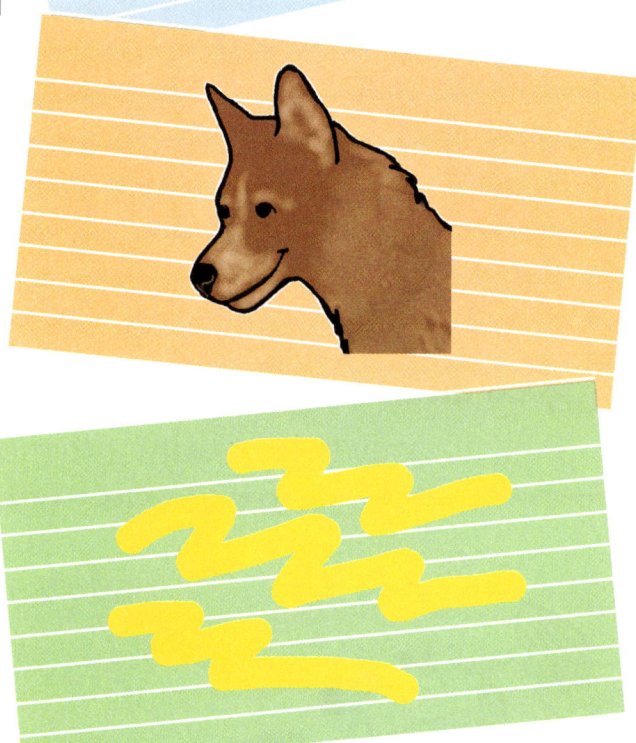

If Chris says yes, you take Chris' brothers card. You put it and your brothers card face up in front of you. Then you get another chance to ask. If Chris says no, you take a card from the Friend Pile. If it matches 1 of yours, you put the pair face up in front of you and take another turn. See who can make the most pairs.

2 Do things with friends. (do both)

☐ **Find things to do.**

Gather magazines and catalogs. Cut out a picture that shows something you would like to do with a friend. Glue it in the first box. Or draw something. In the next box, have a friend glue or draw a picture of something he or she would like to do with you.

☐ **Do an activity.**

Pick an activity to do with a friend, and do it. You may pick one of the ideas from "Find things to do" or one of these:

play a running game

play a board game

play with toys

ride bikes

play with clay

make funny faces

140

3 Meet a new friend.

☐ **Learn how to meet someone new.**

Practice doing these things with someone. Show an adult what you practice.
- Look at the person you'd like to know and smile.
- Say, "Hi," and tell your name.
- Ask what his or her name is.
- Ask him or her to join you in what you are doing.

If you know the person's name, but don't know him or her very well, what else could you say or ask? Role play ideas with a friend.

On the card, write the initials of someone you will try this with in the next week. Think of someone you don't know or someone you'd like to know better.

> **MEET A NEW FRIEND**
>
> I will talk to
>
> _____
>
> this week.

4 Make a snack to share. (do 1)

Get adult help. Ask a friend to join you.

☐ **Decorate cookies.**

Decorate cookies for each other.

☐ **Make caramel apple treats.**

You will need:
- apples
- apple corer or knife
- caramel dip for apples
- toothpicks

Core the apples. Stick toothpicks in the slices. Dip the pieces in the caramel. Eat them!

☐ **Your choice:** _____

5 Be a friend.

☐ **Read or listen to Luke 6:31.**

Use this verse to decide if each sentence shows how to be friend. Circle "yes" if it does. Circle "no" if it doesn't. Explain to an adult how the verse helps you decide.

making fun of my friend	yes	no
sharing with my friend	yes	no
saying bad things about my friend to others	yes	no
playing games my friend likes	yes	no

Extra Credit

☐ Invite a friend to come to Pioneer Clubs with you.

Parents
ACTIVITY AWARD

To earn this award, do the things listed and check off each one:
- ☐ 1. Learn what parents do.
- ☐ 2. Do something special with a parent.
- ☐ 3. God's Word to parents and children.
- ☐ 4. Make a gift for your parent.
- ☐ Extra Credit

Learn what parents do. (do 1)

Act it out.
Your parent does many important things for your family. Act out or more things that your mom or dad does for your family. ave your friends guess what you are acting.

Ask a parent.
Ask your parent what is best about being a parent. rite or draw the answer here.

143

2 Do something special with a parent.

☐ **Invite your parent to do something special with you.**
Make an invitation.
You will need:
- paper (plain and construction paper)
- scissors
- glue
- pictures of adult and child doing things together (cut from magazines or draw your own)
- pencils, crayons, markers
- stickers or other decorations

Your invitation can say things like:

please join me

let's have fun together

a time for just you and me

Write your idea here: _____

Give your invitation to your parent. Decide on what to do. Plan a time to do it. If you can, get a photo of you and your parent at your special event. Show it to your club leader.

3 God's Word to parents and children. *(do both)*

☐ **Read or listen to Colossians 3:20.**
Circle the thing that God wants children to do:

argue   **obey**

Now read or listen to Proverbs 22:6. Circle the thing God asks parents to do:

buy lots of toys   **train children**

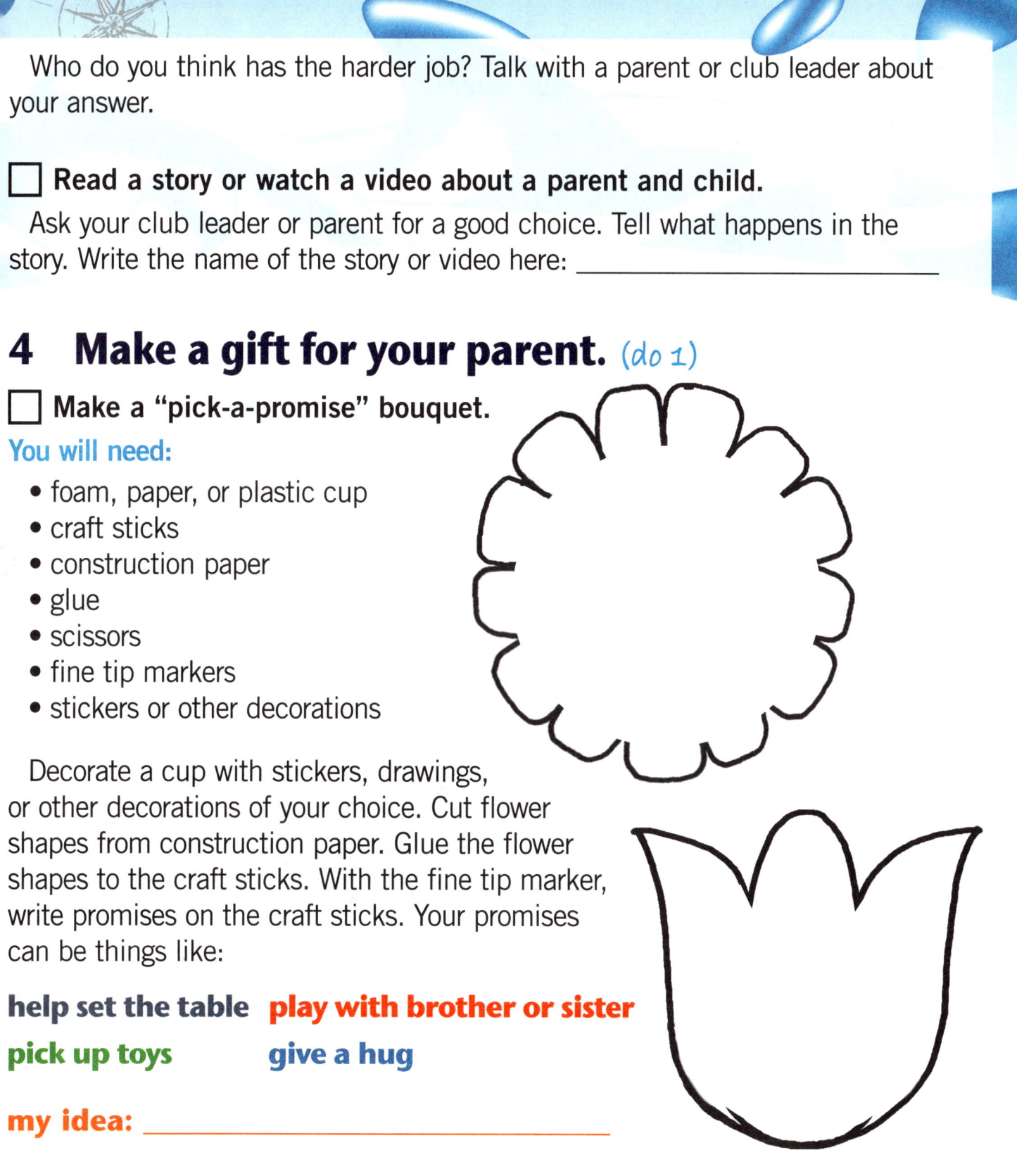

Who do you think has the harder job? Talk with a parent or club leader about your answer.

☐ **Read a story or watch a video about a parent and child.**

Ask your club leader or parent for a good choice. Tell what happens in the story. Write the name of the story or video here: _____

4 Make a gift for your parent. (do 1)

☐ **Make a "pick-a-promise" bouquet.**

You will need:
- foam, paper, or plastic cup
- craft sticks
- construction paper
- glue
- scissors
- fine tip markers
- stickers or other decorations

Decorate a cup with stickers, drawings, or other decorations of your choice. Cut flower shapes from construction paper. Glue the flower shapes to the craft sticks. With the fine tip marker, write promises on the craft sticks. Your promises can be things like:

help set the table   **play with brother or sister**

pick up toys   **give a hug**

my idea: _____

Put your promise flowers in the decorated cup. Give it to a parent. Tell your parent to pick 1 promise at a time. Say that you promise to do the thing he or she picks.

☐ **Make a game to play with your parent.**

Make a tic-tac-toe game.

You will need:

- piece of cardboard 6 by 6 inches (15 by 15 cm)
- piece of felt 6 by 12½ inches (15 by 31 cm)
- 4 6-inch (15 cm) pieces of yarn, in a color different from the felt
- 2 different color pieces of felt, each 1½ by 7½ inches (4 by 18 cm)
- sharp scissors
- glue
- ruler
- fine tip marker

To make the playing board, spread glue on 1 side of the cardboard. Glue it to the large piece of felt. Leave ½ inch (1 cm) of felt sticking out on 1 end. Fold this piece around the cardboard and glue it down.

Put glue on the other edges of the cardboard. Fold the rest of the felt over onto the glue. This makes a pocket to hold the playing pieces.

On the front of the board, measure 2 inches (5 cm) from each edge. Draw lines across to make 9 squares. Glue the yarn over the lines. To make the playing pieces, cut out 5 1-inch (2.5 cm) squares from each color felt.

Extra Credit

☐ Ask your parent about 1 of his or her hobbies. Work together on it. Show your club leader something you did or made.

Safety First
Activity Award

To earn this award, do the things listed and check off each one:
- ☐ 1. Know the signs.
- ☐ 2. Safety rules!
- ☐ 3. Learn what the police do.
- ☐ 4. Play it safe.
- ☐ 5. Be safe with God.

Know the signs.
☐ Match each of these signs with what it means.

You can get out this way.

Don't bike here.

Don't swim here.

Stop and look before driving or biking past the crossroad.

Slow down and look for traffic. Stop if traffic is coming.

Now make up your own safety sign and tell your family or club what it means.

2 Safety rules!

☐ **Make a poster.**

Here are some things you might do that have rules to keep you safe. Talk with an adult about which of the rules would be good for each activity. More than 1 rule might work with each. Make a poster showing good safety rules for 1 of these activities.

Activities:

Crossing a road

Using a computer and the Internet

Catching a ball rolling into the street

Sitting in a car

Riding a bike

Roller skating

Rules:

Have an adult around.

Don't go after it without looking both ways.

Look both ways.

Always wear a seat belt.

Walk across streets.

Wear a helmet.

3 Learn what the police do. (do 1)

☐ **Talk to a police officer.**

Ask the officer about how to be safe at home, at school, and anywhere you go.

☐ **Visit a police department.**

Learn about what different jobs people do there.

☐ **Act out 3 things police officers do.**

4 Play it safe. (do 1)

☐ **Learn road rules.**

Have an adult help you learn the rules of the road for walking safely, beside the road or on sidewalks. Do you know the rules for biking, too? With friends, put on a skit that shows you understand what they mean.

☐ **Learn first aid.**

Have an adult show you how to deal with cuts or scrapes, burns, and insect bites. Learn what to do and who to call if someone is bleeding a lot, has a broken bone, faints, or gets very sick. Role play each of these with friends.

☐ **Look for warnings.**

Find 5 labels on bottles or cans that have warnings. Talk with an adult about what they mean. Make a poster telling kids why to be careful when they see warning labels.

5 Be safe with God.

☐ **Read or listen to Exodus 20:1, 3, 7, 12, 15, 16.**

These are some of God's safety rules. Complete the dot-to-dot to see how you could keep 1 of these rules. Talk with an adult about why following these rules helps keep us safe. Which do you think you need to work on most?

Holidays
Activity Award

To earn this award, do the things listed and check off each one:
- [ ] 1. Learn about a holiday.
- [ ] 2. Make a card.
- [ ] 3. Make a decoration.
- [ ] 4. Make a food.
- [ ] 5. Play holiday games.
- [ ] Extra Credit

1 Learn about a holiday.

- [ ] **Verses**

Read or listen to verses about one of these holidays. Circle what you read.

Christmas	Luke 2:1-7
Easter	Luke 24:1-9
Thanksgiving	1 Chronicles 16:8-9

2 Make a card.

- [ ] **Get creative.**

Choose a holiday. Make a card for someone. Decorate it with glitter glue, stickers, ribbons, construction paper shapes, markers, or whatever you want. *Ideas:*

3 Make a decoration. (do 1)

☐ Horn of Plenty (Thanksgiving)

You will need:

- sugar cone
- small candies
- paper plate
- tube of frosting gel

Use frosting gel to stick a sugar cone to a paper plate. Fill the cone with candy. Use gel to glue each piece in place. Glue some candy spilling out on the plate, too. *Option:* Use the gel to write the name of someone you will give this to on the cone.

☐ Mexican "Tin" Ornament (Christmas)

You will need:

- small disposable pie plate
- marker
- scissors
- scrap cardboard or newspaper
- nail
- string or yarn

Draw a simple shape on the pie plate. Get adult help to cut it out. Set your shape on scrap cardboard or a thick pile of newspaper. Use a large nail to make a hole near the top of the shape. Now use the nail to make dents or holes in a pattern, to decorate the shape. Attach string to the hole to hang your shape.

☐ **Painted Eggs** (Easter)

You will need:
- hard-boiled eggs
- measuring cup and spoons
- white vinegar
- paintbrushes
- food coloring
- water
- small bowls or cups
- smock or old shirt

Wear a smock or old shirt. Mix ¼ cup (60 ml) of water and 1 teaspoon (5 ml) of vinegar in a bowl or cup. Add 15 drops of food coloring. Repeat for each color you want. Paint patterns on the eggs. Let 1 color dry before adding another. Store in the refrigerator.

☐ Your Choice: _____

4 Make a food.

☐ **Holiday Food**

Does your family have foods you always eat for Thanksgiving, Christmas, or Easter? Ask for help to make one of those foods.

Ideas:

Thanksgiving: pumpkin pie, pumpkin bread, cranberry sauce

Christmas: gingerbread, fancy cookies

Easter: hot cross buns, colored eggs

I made: _____

Here's what I thought of what I made:

☐ Yummy!   ☐ So-so   ☐ No seconds, please.

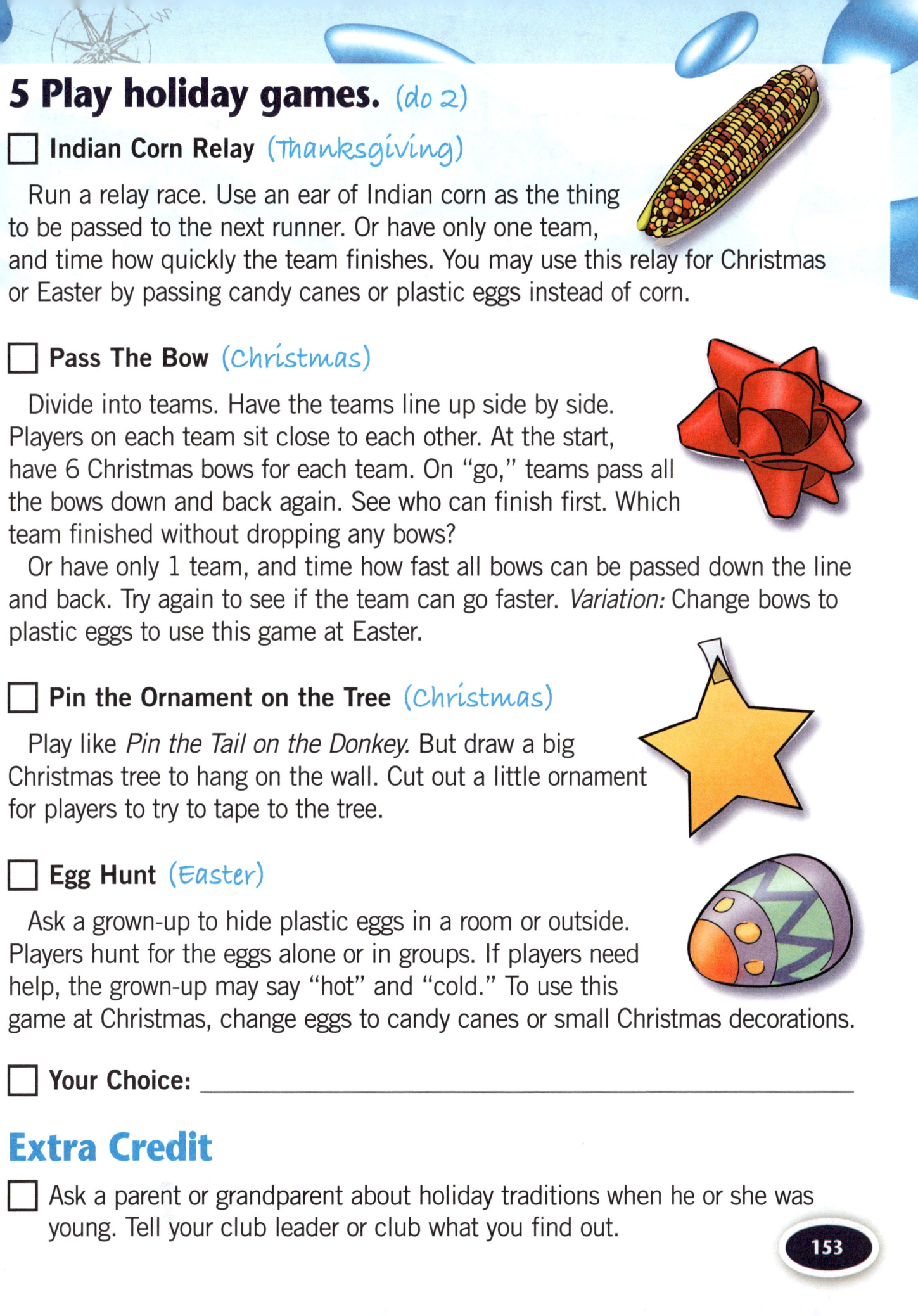

5 Play holiday games. (do 2)

☐ **Indian Corn Relay** (Thanksgiving)

Run a relay race. Use an ear of Indian corn as the thing to be passed to the next runner. Or have only one team, and time how quickly the team finishes. You may use this relay for Christmas or Easter by passing candy canes or plastic eggs instead of corn.

☐ **Pass The Bow** (Christmas)

Divide into teams. Have the teams line up side by side. Players on each team sit close to each other. At the start, have 6 Christmas bows for each team. On "go," teams pass all the bows down and back again. See who can finish first. Which team finished without dropping any bows?

Or have only 1 team, and time how fast all bows can be passed down the line and back. Try again to see if the team can go faster. *Variation:* Change bows to plastic eggs to use this game at Easter.

☐ **Pin the Ornament on the Tree** (Christmas)

Play like *Pin the Tail on the Donkey*. But draw a big Christmas tree to hang on the wall. Cut out a little ornament for players to try to tape to the tree.

☐ **Egg Hunt** (Easter)

Ask a grown-up to hide plastic eggs in a room or outside. Players hunt for the eggs alone or in groups. If players need help, the grown-up may say "hot" and "cold." To use this game at Christmas, change eggs to candy canes or small Christmas decorations.

☐ Your Choice: _____

Extra Credit

☐ Ask a parent or grandparent about holiday traditions when he or she was young. Tell your club leader or club what you find out.

Nature Craft
Activity Award

To earn this award, do the things listed and check off each one:
- ☐ 1. Make nature crafts.
- ☐ 2. Respond to Psalm 24:1.
- ☐ Extra Credit

1 Make nature crafts. (do 3)

☐ **Make a nature scrapbook.**

You will need:
- construction paper
- scissors
- hole punch
- twine or yarn
- nature items or nature pictures from magazines
- glue
- markers

Cut several pieces of construction paper in half. Use a hole punch to make 2 holes on one edge, at the same places on each page. Use twine or yarn to tie the pages together. Decorate the front of your scrapbook with a nature picture that you draw or cut out. Collect leaves, flowers, and other nature items. Glue them on the pages.

☐ **Make a rock paperweight.**

You will need:
- medium-sized rock
- crayons
- metal pan covered with foil
- old sock or other soft rag
- oven mitts
- oven

> **!** Have an adult help whenever you use an oven.
> Use oven mitts when moving things into or out of a hot oven.

Have an adult help you set the oven to 200° F (95° C).

Pick a smooth rock with a flat side. Color it with crayons. Using lots of crayon will make your paperweight look better. Place the colored rock on a foil-covered pan. Put the pan in the oven for 15 minutes. Take the pan out. Let the rock cool for at least 5 minutes. Test how warm the rock is by holding your hand above it for a few seconds before you pick it up.

When your rock is cool, rub it with an old sock or other soft rag to make the rock look shiny.

☐ Make a stick vase.

You will need:
- sticks about ¼ inch (6 mm) thick
- empty plastic jar
- scissors
- glue
- 2 rubber bands
- raffia or ribbon
- pinecones or other nature items

Break or cut the sticks to about an inch (25 mm) taller than the jar. Put 2 rubber bands around the jar, about an inch (25 mm) from the top and the bottom. Tuck the sticks under the rubber bands. Push the sticks close together.

Now tie raffia or ribbon around the jar to hide the rubber bands. Glue on nature items. Use your jar to hold flowers, pencils, or any small items.

☐ **Make a nature placemat.**

You will need:
- 2 sheets of sticky-backed clear plastic
- scissors
- leaves, flowers, or other flat nature items
- construction paper

Put your construction paper on the sticky side of 1 sheet of plastic. Your paper should be slightly smaller than the plastic. Arrange leaves, flowers, and other nature items on the construction paper. If a flower is thick, take off the petals, and use them separately. Cover with the other sheet of plastic. Trim the edges so they are all even.

☐ **Your Choice:** _____

2 Respond to Psalm 24:1.

☐ **Be glad.**

You will need:
- markers
- plain paper
- cardboard or posterboard
- nature items such as acorns, pinecones, pods, twigs, sand
- tacky glue

Read or listen to Psalm 24:1. Look at the next page. Circle the things in nature that you are glad God made. Draw your own idea on another piece of paper. Glue your picture to a piece of cardboard that's at least 1 inch (25 mm) bigger than the picture on all sides. Glue nature items onto the cardboard frame to cover it.

Extra Credit

☐ Find things in your home that were made from things in nature. Tell your club leader what you find.

Puppets
ACTIVITY AWARD

To earn this award, do the things listed and check off each one:
- ☐ 1. Pick a story.
- ☐ 2. Make puppets.
- ☐ 3. Make a stage.
- ☐ 4. God directs our story.
- ☐ 5. Tell a story.
- ☐ Extra Credit

1 Pick a story.

☐ **Decide what puppets to make.**

Find a Bible story you like, make up a story, or use a story from a book. You will make puppets to tell this story.

2 Make puppets. (do 1)

☐ **Fuzzy Wire Faces**

You will need:
- chenille wire (pipe cleaners) in different colors
- large wiggle craft eyes
- tacky glue
- ruler

Wrap the middle of the wire around your finger and twist the ends. This makes a loop in the middle.

About an inch (2.5 cm) from the first loop, twist a smaller loop on each half of the wire. The picture shows this. Glue a craft eye to each smaller loop.

Bend the rest of the wire to make eyebrows. Or attach other chenille wires to add details like hair, a hat, glasses, or ears.

Slide the puppet on your finger to use it.

☐ **Tube Heads**

You will need:

- cardboard tube from toilet paper, paper towel, or gift wrap
- scissors
- ruler
- construction paper, felt, or cloth
- colored markers
- glue
- optional: wiggle eyes, decorations

You need a piece of a cardboard tube about 2 inches (5 cm) long for each head you make. Have a grownup help you cut this. Cover the sides and 1 end of the tube with cloth or paper. Draw a face with markers. Use more paper or cloth to add hair or animal ears.

To use, put the puppet on your middle 2 or 3 fingers. Use your thumb and little finger as the puppet's arms. Wear knit gloves to give the puppet a sweater.

☐ **Spoon Family**

You will need:

- set of metal measuring spoons, large craft sticks, or wooden spoons
- light color opaque paint markers
- black fine-tip permanent marker
- scissors
- tacky glue
- construction paper
- felt or cloth scraps
- yarn

Measuring spoons give you large and small head sizes, so you can have grownups and children.

Paint the back of a spoon any light color. Draw a face with the black marker. Glue paper or cloth around the handle for clothing. Glue paper or yarn hair around the face.

☐ **Your Choice:** _____

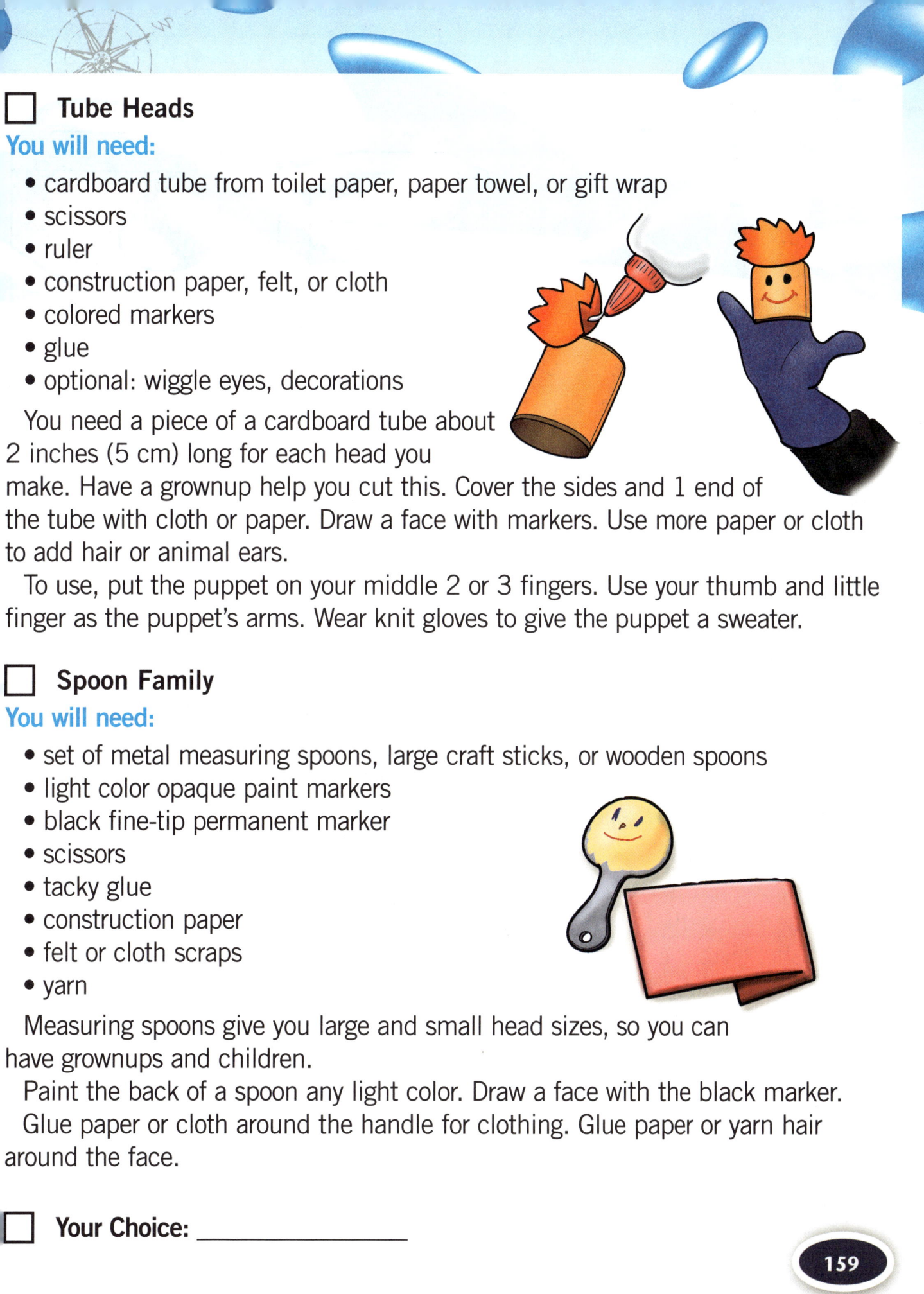

3 Make a stage. (do 1)

☐ **Cardboard Box Stage**

You will need:

- cardboard box
- glue
- paint, paintbrushes
- markers
- optional: string, paper, or cloth

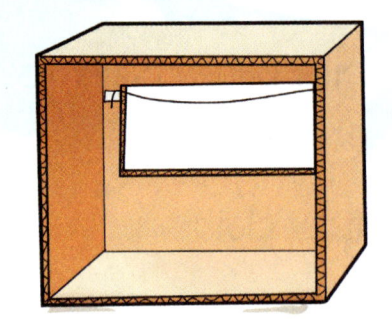

Draw a window on the side of the box facing the opening. Have a grownup help you cut it out. Paint the box. Decorate with markers. Look at the picture to see how you can hang curtains from a string running through the box just above the opening. You may also hang a paper or cloth backdrop at the back.

☐ **Curtain Stage**

You will need:

- 2 matching chairs with straight backs
- broomstick or other long rod
- cloth
- optional: string or tape, safety pins

Put chairs next to each other, backs together. Put the broomstick across the chair backs. If the stick rolls, use string or tape to keep it in place.

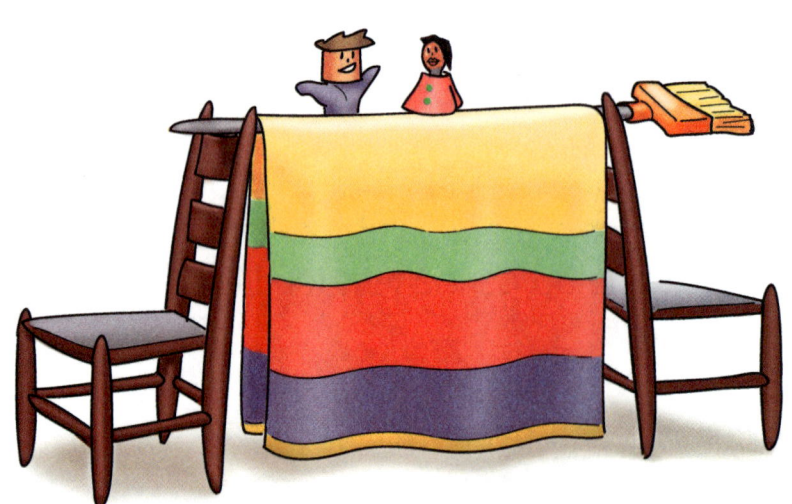

Drape a cloth over the broomstick so it reaches the floor. Safety pins can help hold the cloth in place.

☐ **Your Choice:** _____

4 God directs our story.

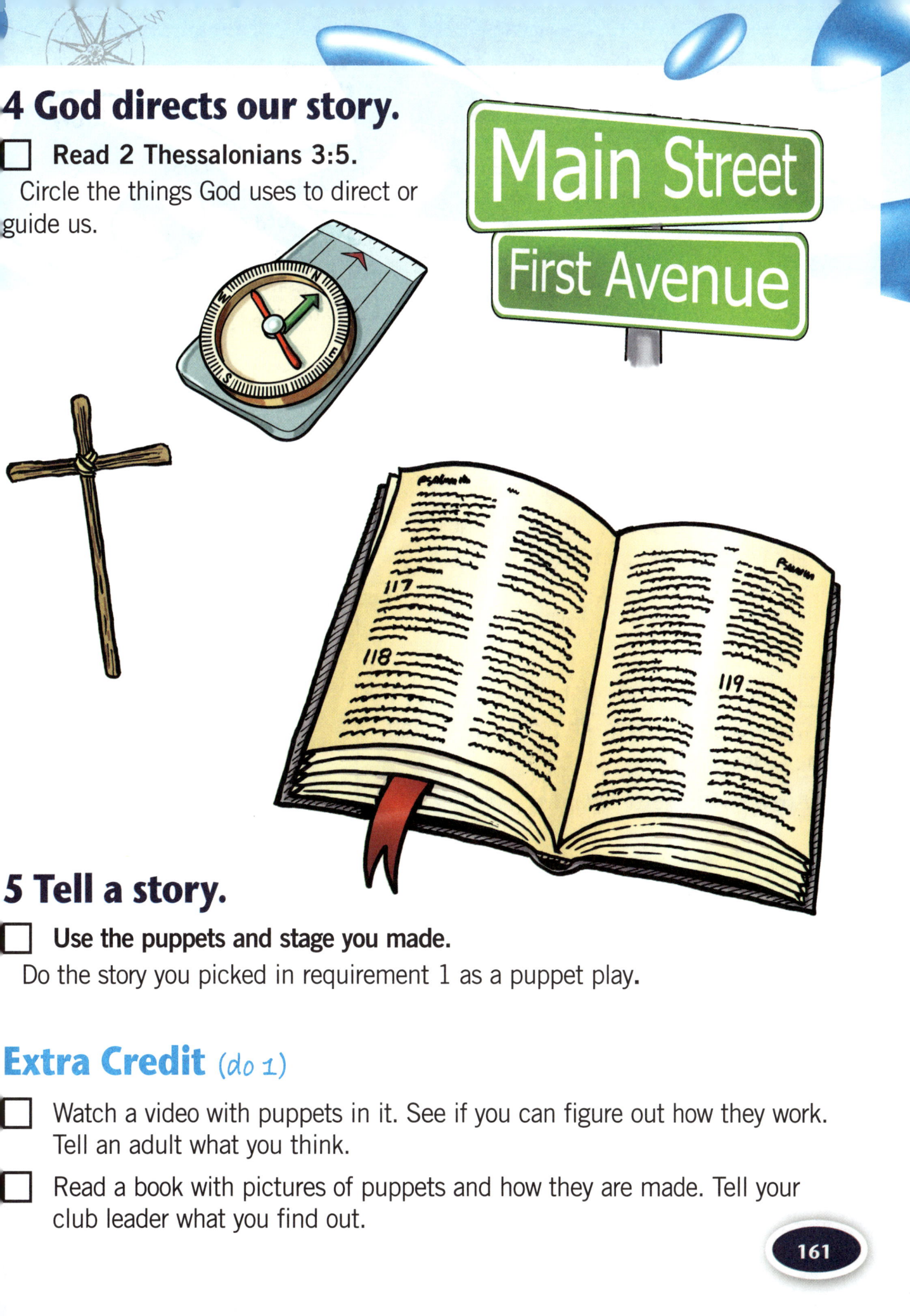

☐ **Read 2 Thessalonians 3:5.**

Circle the things God uses to direct or guide us.

5 Tell a story.

☐ **Use the puppets and stage you made.**

Do the story you picked in requirement 1 as a puppet play.

Extra Credit (do 1)

☐ Watch a video with puppets in it. See if you can figure out how they work. Tell an adult what you think.

☐ Read a book with pictures of puppets and how they are made. Tell your club leader what you find out.

Puzzles
ACTIVITY AWARD

To earn this award, do the things listed and check off each one:
- ☐ 1. Move the Lines
- ☐ 2. Tangram
- ☐ 3. Word Chains
- ☐ 4. Connected to God
- ☐ 5. Jigsaw Puzzle
- ☐ Extra Credit

1 Move the Lines (do both)

☐ **Play with straw squares.**

Start with 12 straws placed as shown. Mark which 2 you can take away to have only 2 squares left.

Hint: These straws form 5 squares now.

☐ **Play with straw fish.**

Move 3 straws to make a fish swimming the other direction.

Answers at end of award.

2 Tangram

☐ **Make shapes.**

You will need:
- cardboard
- scissors
- glue
- copy of tangram pattern

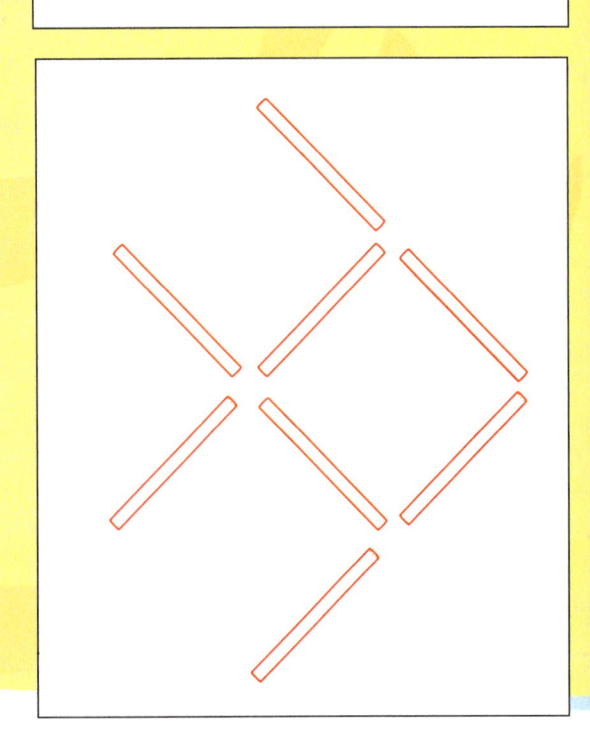

Glue the tangram pattern on your cardboard. Cut out the individual shapes. Put the pieces back together as a square without looking at this page. Now arrange the pieces to match the candle design. Use all 7 shapes. Do not overlap them. (Answer at end of award.) Make some designs of your own. Trace 1 you really like and color it in.

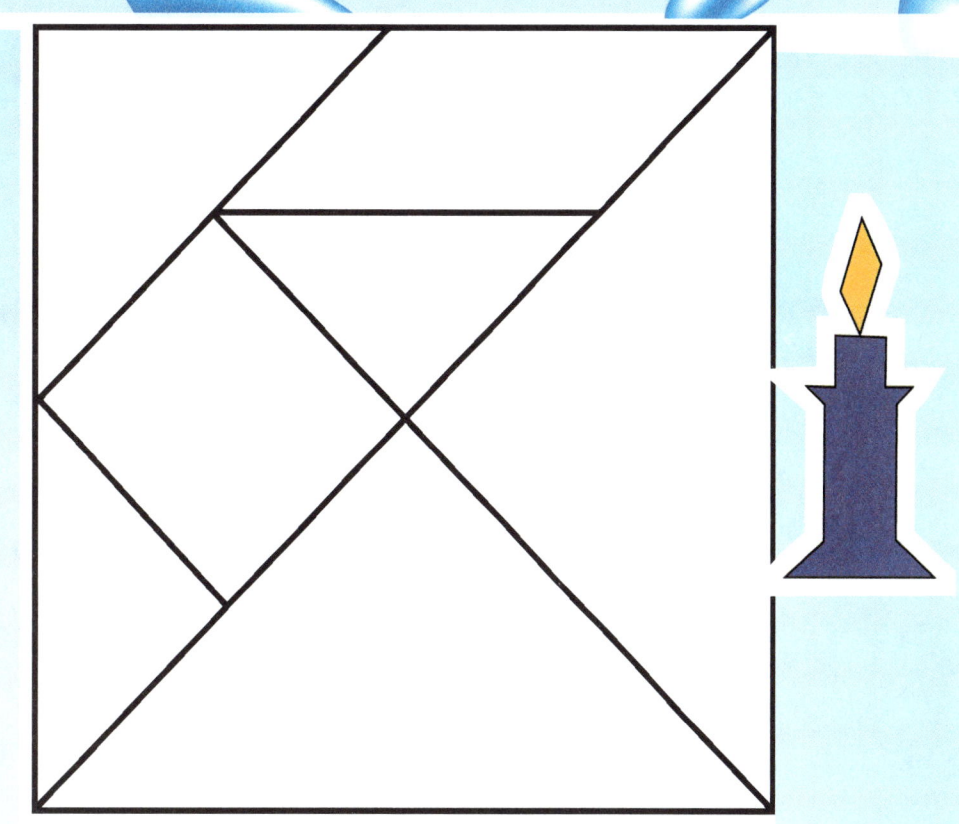

Pattern may be reproduced for use with Pioneer Clubs® Voyager materials.

3 Word Chains

☐ **Fill in the blanks.**

Fill in the blanks with letters to make the words in these word chain puzzles. *Hint:* Look at how letters change on the next line down.

Put this nap to bed.

N	A	P	
_	A	P	plant juice
S	A	_	not happy
_	A	D	not good
B	E	D	

Make a tree grow from a seed.

S	E	E	D	
_	E	E	D	give food
F	_	E	D	boy's name
F	R	E	_	not caught
T	R	E	E	

163

Make a chain from God to you.

G	O	D	
G	O	_	I ____ a gift on my birthday.
G	_	T	I will ___ a gift next year, too.
_	E	T	in a bit, not _____
Y	E	_	evergreen bush with red berries
Y	_	W	noise meaning "ouch"
Y	O	U	

4 Connected to God

☐ Read or listen to Hebrews 1:1.
Solve this puzzle:

Before, God spoke to his people through
___ ___ ___ ___ ___ ___ ___ ___.
5   6   4   5   2   1   8   7

Now God speaks to us through his ___ ___ ___.
                                   7   4   3

E = 1   H = 2   N = 3   O = 4
P = 5   R = 6   S = 7   T = 8

164

5 Jigsaw Puzzle

☐ **Do a jigsaw puzzle.**
Choose a puzzle with at least 50 pieces.

Extra Credit

☐ Put together a jigsaw puzzle with 250 or more pieces with your family or friends.

Solution to Move the Lines:

Take 2 sticks out of the middle, as marked in red.

Move the three sticks shown in grey above the fish shape as shown in black, to create a fish going the other way.

Solution to candle tangram:

Science Fun
ACTIVITY AWARD

To earn this award, do the things listed and check off each one:
- ☐ 1. Which holds more?
- ☐ 2. Make something get bigger.
- ☐ 3. Look closely!
- ☐ 4. Have fun with a mirror.

1 Which holds more?

☐ **How much does each hold?**

You will need:
- tall, narrow glass or jar
- shorter, wider glass or jar
- 2-cup (500 ml) measuring cup
- water
- sink or large basin
- other shapes and sizes of glasses, bottles, or jars

Look at your tall and short containers. Circle the picture most like the one you think will hold more water.

Tall

Wide

Fill each with water. Carefully pour the water from the taller one into the measuring cup. How much did it hold? _____

Do the same with the shorter, wider one. How much did it hold? _____

Which holds more? _____

Did you guess right? 😊 😟 **(circle 1)**

Compare some more glasses, bottles and jars. Look for ones with slanting or curved sides. Are you surprised at how much or how little they hold?

2 Make something get bigger. (do 1)

☐ Make a tasty explosion.

You will need:
- popcorn popper
- water
- strainer or colander
- ⅔ cup unpopped popcorn
- measuring cup
- shallow bowl
- clean towel

Soak ⅓ cup (100 ml) of the popcorn in a bowl of water for 30 minutes.

Pop ⅓ cup (100 ml) of dry popcorn in your popper. Count the unpopped pieces. Drain the popcorn that you soaked. Pat it dry on a towel. Pop it. Count the unpopped pieces.

Which popcorn had fewer unpopped pieces? **Wet Dry (circle 1)**

Here's why: Each kernel of popcorn has some water in it. When you heat popcorn, the water turns to steam and makes the kernel explode. Kernels that don't pop are too dry. Soaking in water for 30 minutes gives too-dry kernels enough water to pop.

☐ Make a coin tap dance.

You will need:
- empty 2-liter plastic soda bottle
- quarter or larger coin
- water
- freezer

Take the top off the empty bottle. Put the bottle in the freezer for 10 minutes.

Dip the coin in water. Remove the bottle from the freezer. Right away, put the wet coin on top of the bottle.

What happens?_____

Here's why: In the freezer, the air inside the bottle got cold. As that air warms up, it takes up more space and pushes out of the bottle, making the coin bounce up for a moment. When the coin falls down, it clicks against the bottle top. The air in the bottle warms some more, and the coin hops again.

☐ **Pop your top—slowly!**

You will need:
- small plastic storage container with a snap-on top
- cold water
- freezer
- sink or large basin

Fill the container with cold water over a sink or basin. Fill until it overflows. Carefully snap the lid on. You don't want any air inside at all. Put it in the freezer. Wait a few hours for all the water to freeze.

Check your container. Draw or write down what you see.

Here's why: Water takes up more space when it turns to ice.

3 Look closely!

☐ **Eye Teasers**

You will need a ruler! First, pick your answer. Use your ruler to check it out.

Arrows Inside and Out: Which center line is longest? _____

Here's why: Your brain judges the lengths of the straight lines by the total length of each arrow. So the top line looks shortest and the bottom longest.

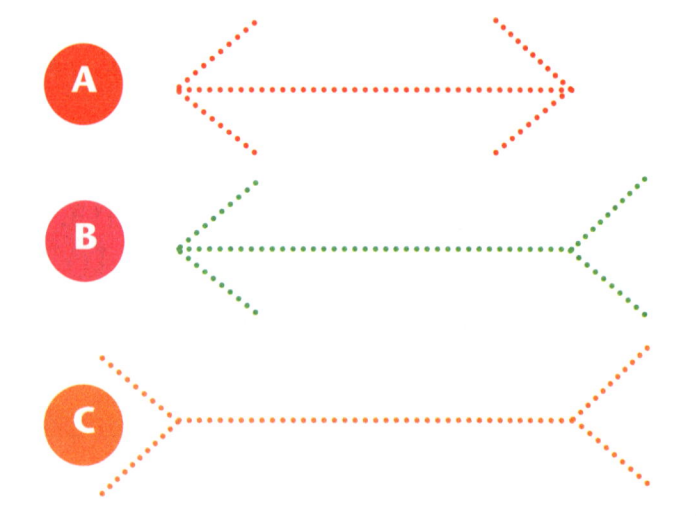

Tricky Circles: Which center circle is bigger?

1   2   (circle your choice)

Use your ruler to check.

Here's why: Both center circles are the same size. But center circle #1 is bigger than the little ones around it. So you think it's bigger than center circle #2, which is smaller than the circles around it.

Squashed Square: Are the sides of the blue square curved?

Yes   **No**   (circle 1)

Here's why: The circles make your brain think the straight lines crossing them must also curve.

Flat or Tilting? Do the lines between these rows of black and white patches tilt?

Yes   **No**   (circle 1)

Here's why: The black squares form V shapes top to bottom. This confuses your brain, so the lines going straight across seem to tilt.

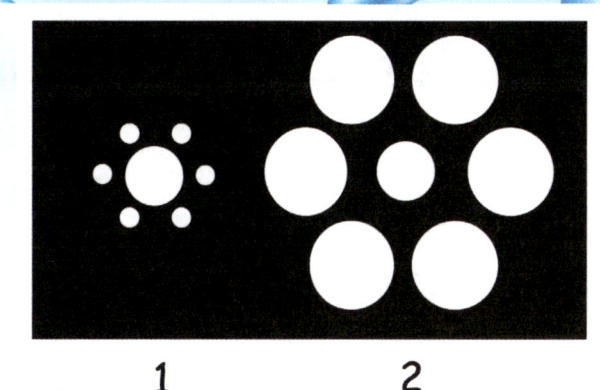

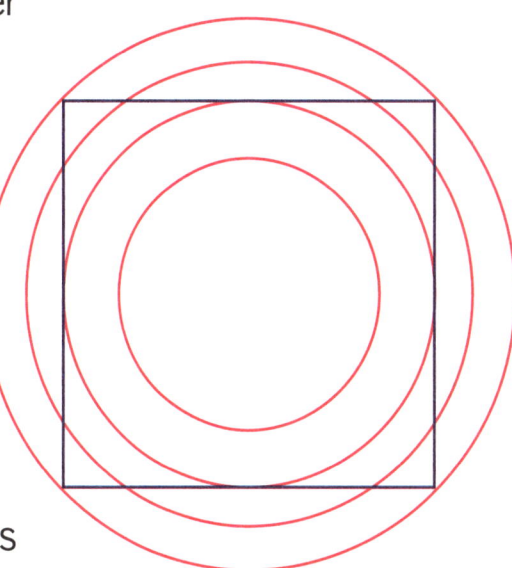

4 Have fun with a mirror.

(do 2)

☐ Fool Your Hand

Draw a big curvy shape. Try to draw over that shape. Circle what happened:

I stayed close to the curve I drew.
I had a hard time following the curve.

Set up your paper by a mirror as shown. Looking only in the mirror, try to draw over the curve. Circle what happened:

I stayed close to the curve.   **I had a hard time following the curve.**

Here's why: Tracing the curve is hard because you see your hand move in reverse.

☐ Who's That?

You will need:
- small, unframed mirror
- photo of yourself looking straight ahead

Look at the picture. Put the mirror on your photo like that. Now flip the mirror over so it shows the other side of your face.

Circle which looks more like you.

The left side and its reflection

The right side and its reflection

Here's why: We have 2 eyes and ears with a nose and mouth along the middle. But the left and right sides of a face are slightly different. So half of your face and its mirror image can look quite unlike your whole face.

☐ Hall of Mirrors

Hold 2 mirrors facing each other. Move 1 side of 1 mirror closer or farther away—what happens?

Here's why: An image appears farther away when it reflects in a mirror. So the facing mirrors make what looks like doorways leading down a long hall.

Stitch and Sew
Activity Award

To earn this award, do the things listed and check off each one:
- ☐ 1. Learn the basics.
- ☐ 2. Practice some stitches.
- ☐ 3. Make a project.
- ☐ Extra Credit

Learn the basics. (do all)

You will need:
- thread
- scissors
- needle
- cloth scrap

Have an adult show you how to do each of these things.

- ☐ Thread a needle.
- ☐ Tie a knot to hold the thread.
- ☐ Do running stitches.
- ☐ Do overcast stitching.

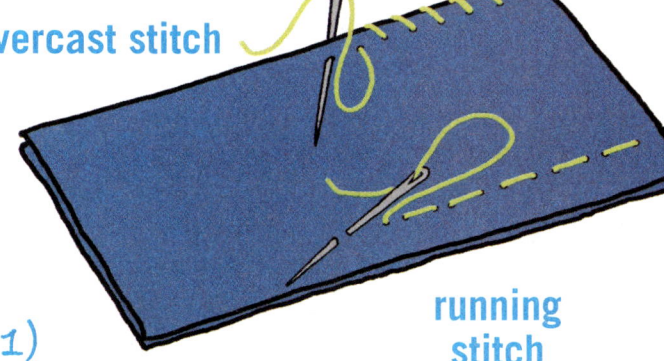

overcast stitch

running stitch

Practice some stitches. (do 1)

- ☐ Bookmark

You will need:
- embroidery thread
- embroidery needle
- scissors
- felt, 2 by 6 inches (5 by 15 cm)

Use the running stitch to make a design on the bookmark. If you like, use the overcast stitch to decorate the edges.

171

☐ **Bandanna**

You will need:
- colorful fabric (lightweight cotton or cotton-blend)
- scissors
- ruler or tape measure
- straight pins
- iron and ironing board
- thread
- needle

Cut the fabric into a square 24½ inches (62 cm) on a side. Fold each edge ¼ inch (6 mm). Have an adult help you press a straight fold with an iron. Fold each pressed edge in; pin and press again. The cut edge should now be hidden inside the folds. Use overcast or running stitches to sew th folds down.

☐ **Your Choice:** _____

3 Make a project. (do 1)

☐ **Christmas Ornament**

You will need:
- felt
- scissors
- ruler
- needle
- thread
- ribbon
- optional: buttons, sequins

Cut out 2 copies of a Christmas shape. You might make a circle, star, or tree. Cut 6 inches (15 cm) of ribbon. Fold it in half. Sew the cut ends to the top of your shapes as shown. This is the hanger. Sew the shapes' edge together using the overcast stitch. Sew on other felt pieces and ribbon to make the ornament fancy. *Option:* Sew or glue on buttons and sequins.

☐ **Glasses or Pencil Case**

You will need:
- colorful thick fabric
- scissors
- ruler
- straight pins
- thread
- needle
- iron and ironing board

Cut 2 pieces of fabric, 5½ by 7 inches (14 by 18 cm). Pin the 2 pieces of fabric together, right sides inside. Do a running stitch ¼ inch (6 mm) from the edge around 3 sides to form a pocket. Leave 1 short side open. Turn the fabric inside out. Have an adult help you iron the seams flat.

Fold the cut edges on the open side to the inside of the pocket. Make the folds ¼ inch (6 mm) wide. Press flat. Pin the open end. Sew it closed with the overhand stitch. Fold the fabric in half as the picture shows. Pin the long side across from the fold and the end without stitching showing. Sew the sides you have pinned.

☐ **Your Choice:** _____

Extra Credit (do 1)

☐ Learn to sew on a snap or button.
☐ Ask someone who sews clothing or quilts what he or she enjoys about sewing.

Tools
Activity Award

To earn this award, do the things listed and check off each one:
- [ ] 1. Learn to cut.
- [ ] 2. Learn to build.
- [ ] 3. Make something.
- [ ] 4. Do things for God.
- [ ] Extra Credit

1 Learn to cut. (do both)

- [ ] **Saw a board.**
- [ ] **Drill a hole.**

Draw lines from the pictures of the tools you used to what you did.

Never use tools without a grownup present!

2 Learn to build. (do 2)

Draw lines from the pictures of the tools you used to what you used them on.

- ☐ Pound in a nail and take it out again.
- ☐ Tighten a screw.
- ☐ Put a nut on a bolt and take it off.

3 Make something. (do 1)

☐ **Calendar Cubes**

You will need:
- scrap wood, to cut into 2 matching cubes
- sandpaper
- saw
- clean rag
- 2 colors of paint
- large and small paintbrush
- optional: stick-on numbers or number stencils

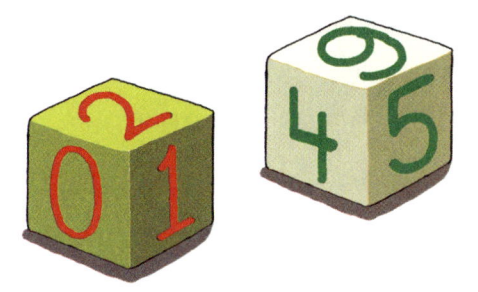

Cubes should be bigger than 1½ inches (4 cm) on a side.

Have a grownup help you cut the wood cubes. Sand the wood smooth. Wipe off any dust. Paint the wood a color you like. Let the cubes dry. Paint or stick on a number on each side of each cube. One cube should have the numbers 1, 2, 3, 4, 5, and 6. The other should have 0, 1, 2, 3, 7, and 8. The 6 can be turned upside down for a 9.

☐ **Book Stand**

You will need:

- 1 x 6 board, 24 inches (60 cm) long
- pencil
- ruler
- saw
- 5 finish nails
- dowel rod, 5 inches (13 cm) long and 1 inch (25 mm) in diameter
- drill
- wood glue
- hammer

3/8 inch (1 cm) from edge

Measure 9 inches (23 cm) from 1 end of the board and mark. Cut the board into 2 pieces at the mark.

Drill 3 holes along 1 end of the shorter board, as shown. Put glue on the end of the long board. Nail the short board to the end of the long board.

Drill 2 holes in the dowel, an inch (2.5 cm) from each end. Nail the dowel to the bottom of the shelf 3 inches (7.5 cm) from the other end of the long board.

☐ **Your Choice:** _____

4 Do things for God.

☐ **Read or listen to 1 Kings 6:14-15.**

What kinds of workers did King Solomon need when he built the temple for God?

The people building the temple made smaller things, too. They made doors and carved pictures. What can you make or do with tools at church for God?

☐ Help paint.

☐ Help clear brush or fallen branches.

☐ Help hang a picture.

☐ My idea: _____

Extra Credit (do 1)

☐ Have a parent help you use a tool to fix something around your home.

☐ Visit a carpenter's shop. Ask what he or she likes best about being a carpenter.

Animals
ACTIVITY AWARD

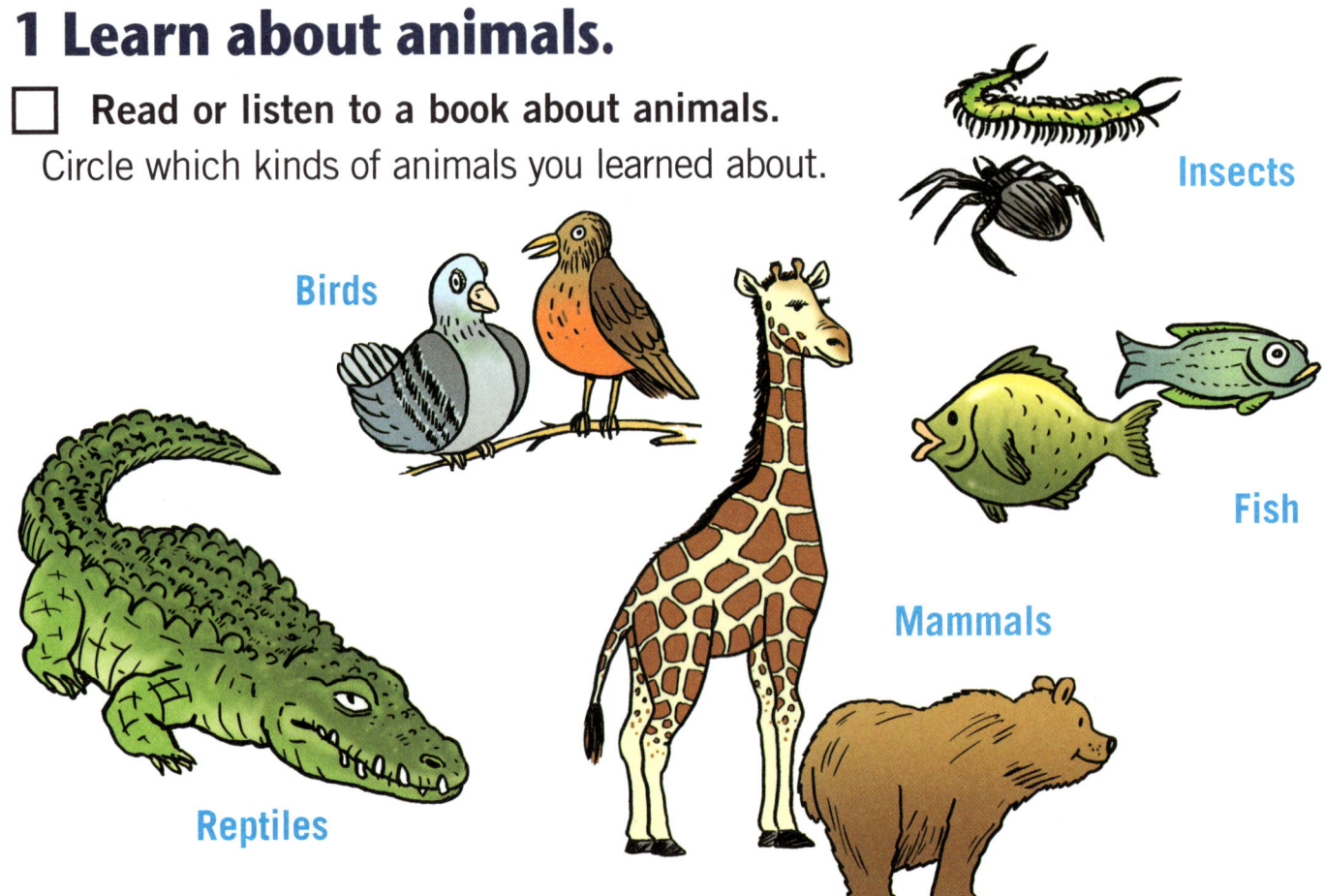

To earn this award, do the things listed and check off each one:
- ☐ 1. Learn about animals.
- ☐ 2. Play an animal game.
- ☐ 3. Meet an animal.
- ☐ 4. Know God feeds animals.
- ☐ 5. Help God feed animals.
- ☐ 6. Do an animal project.

1 Learn about animals.

☐ **Read or listen to a book about animals.**
Circle which kinds of animals you learned about.

Insects

Birds

Fish

Mammals

Reptiles

2 Play an animal game. (do 1)

☐ **Animal Charades**
   Players take turns acting out different pets, farm animals, or zoo creatures while others try to guess what each is. The first person with a correct guess who has not already been an animal gets to act out an animal next.

☐ Octopus Tag

Choose a playing area. The sides are the "shores." In between is the "ocean." IT—the "octopus"—stands in the middle of the ocean. The other players, or "fish," stand by 1 shore. When IT yells, "Octopus!" all the fish "swim" to the other shore. IT tries to tag them. Players who are tagged must stay where they were tagged. In the next round, they also tag runners. But they may not move their feet. The last player tagged is the next IT.

☐ Who Am I?

Each player gets a tag on his or her back with the name of an animal. Players must figure out what their animal is by asking other players questions that can be answered yes or no, such as "Am I a pet?" or "Do I fly?"

☐ Find the Cowbell

Players form a circle. One player is the cow. The cow stands in the middle, blindfolded. The others pass a bell (the "cowbell"). Each player must ring it and pass it along. When the cow says, "Moo," the next player rings the bell but does not pass it along. The cow gets 3 tries to point to the person with the cowbell. The player holding the bell becomes the new cow.

☐ Your Choice: _____

3 Meet an animal. (do 1)

☐ Pet

Ask someone to introduce a new pet to you. Or visit a pet store. Learn 1 way to take care of the pet. Try it out, or act it out. Draw the pet you met.

☐ **Bugs**
Go outside. Use a magnifying glass. Look under logs or rocks. Or look near a light at night. How many kinds of bugs did you see? _____

☐ **Farm Animal**
Visit a farm or county fair. Find out what 1 animal eats. Write it on the barn.

☐ **Zoo Animal**
Visit a zoo or petting zoo. Feed an animal, if you're allowed to. Circle what 1 animal feels like or looks like.

Animal: _____

soft   rough   smooth   prickly   hard

4 Know God feeds animals.

☐ **Read or listen to Psalm 104:24, 27.**
Fill in the blanks in this sentence by unscrambling the letters underneath.

God made both __ __ __ __ __ __ __
                M I A S N L A

and their __ __ __ __.
           O D O F

5 Help God feed animals. (do 1)

☐ **Hanging Peanut Treat**

You will need:
- string
- peanuts in the shell

Use 3 feet (1 m) of string. Leave 4 inches (10 cm) free at the top. Then tie on a peanut. About 2 inches (5 cm) lower, tie on another peanut. Keep tying peanuts on until you fill your string. Tie your feeder onto a branch for birds to enjoy.

☐ **Critter Wreath**

You will need:
- #18 galvanized wire
- wire cutters
- goggles
- metal file
- pliers
- dried or fresh fruit, day-old bread, dried corn on the cob cut in sections

Have a grownup cut 26 inches (66 cm) of wire and file down any sharp edges. Poke the wire through pieces of food. Leave some wire empty on both ends. Have an adult help you use pliers to bend each end into a hook. Bend the wire into a circle. Hook the ends together. Hang your wreath on a bush or tree branch. Clean off any rotten fruit every 2 or 3 days.

☐ **Easy Finch Feeder**

You will need:
- pantyhose or stockings
- 12 inches (30 cm) of ribbon
- ruler
- scissors
- 2 cups (500 ml) thistle seeds
- measuring cup

Measure 8 to 10 inches (20 to 25 cm) up from the toe end of an old pair of pantyhose or other see-through stockings. Cut across the hose there to get a bag. Pour in thistle seeds. Tie a knot in the top of the stocking bag. Tie a loop in your ribbon. Tie the ends of the ribbon around the knot at the top of your bird feeder. Use the loop to hang your feeder outside a window where you can watch the birds that come.

☐ Your Choice: _____

6 Do an animal project. (do 1)

☐ **Pom-Pom Teddy Bear**

You will need:
- 1 large pom-pom
- 1 medium pom-pom
- 5 small pom-poms
- 3 extra-small pom-poms
- small black bead
- tacky glue
- 2 wiggle eyes

Glue your bear together as shown.

☐ **Money or Supplies**

Call an animal shelter to learn what they need. Make a poster showing what you want to collect. Hang it in church. Ask people to donate. Take what you collect to the shelter.

☐ **Care**

Help care for an animal for a week.

☐ Your Choice: _____

Campfire
ACTIVITY AWARD

To earn this award, do the things listed and check off each one:

☐ 1. Play learning games.
☐ 2. Help build a fire.
☐ 3. Have fun around your fire.
☐ 4. Cook on your fire.
☐ 5. Remember God.
☐ 6. Help put out a fire.

1 Play learning games. (do both)

☐ **Safety Crossword**
Do the puzzle to find ways to keep safe with a campfire.

WORD LIST

close
bucket
adult
build
bigger
hands
leave

Across
1. ____ the fire in the firepit, if there is one.
5. Do not poke the fire with your ____ or feet.
6. Don't pile wood ____ to the fire.
7. Do not build a ____ fire than you need.

Down
2. Do not ____ the area while the fire is burning.
3. Always have an ____ help you.
4. Keep a ____ of water close by.

Answers at the end of the award.

183

☐ **Sorting Game**

Match the sentences with the right pictures.

Tinder catches fire easily from a match.

Kindling is bigger sticks that catch fire from the tinder.

Fuel is big wood that burns a long time.

Now play a game. The game leader collects lots of tinder, kindling, and fuel. He or she mixes it all up together. On "Go," sort the items into 3 piles: tinder, kindling, and fuel.

2 Help build a fire.

☐ **Learn where the wood goes.**

Have an adult help you pile up tinder and kindling. Tinder goes on first. Kindling comes next. Let the adult light the fire and add fuel.

3 Have fun around your fire. (do 1)

☐ **Sing songs.**

Sing some camp songs or hiking songs. Sing some praise songs to God.

☐ **Tell a story.**

Use 1 of these story titles. Or think of your own. Everyone could think of things to add to the story as you go.

Raccoons Visit the Voyager Campfire

Mystery in the Voyager Club Room

My Dog, the Slob

☐ **Tell jokes.**

☐ **Play a game.**

Here's an idea.

> **Drip, Drip, Drop**
>
> Play like *Duck, Duck, Goose,* sitting in a circle. But the person who's IT carries a cup with a little water in it. Instead of tapping players and saying, "Duck," IT says, "Drip." On "Drop," IT dumps the water. Then IT runs around the circle while the wet player tries to tag IT before IT can sit in the empty spot. Be sure to play far enough away from the campfire that no one could fall and get burned!

4 Cook on your fire. (do 1)

Have an adult help you.

☐ **Easy Brown Bears**

Roll a piece of hot dog bun in melted butter. Then roll it in cinnamon and sugar. Wrap it in foil. Cook in coals for about 5 minutes, turning often.

☐ **S'Mores**

Toast a marshmallow. Put it between graham crackers with a piece of chocolate bar.

☐ **Soup**

Use a pot on a grill rack. Heat some soup.

☐ **Egg in a Cup**

Find a wax-covered paper cup just a little bigger than an egg. Put in the egg. Fill the cup with water. Have an adult put the cup near the coals. Don't worry if the top of the cup catches fire. Let the water boil long enough to cook the egg. Have an adult use tongs to remove the cup from the fire.

☐ **Your Choice:** _____

5 Remember God.

☐ **Read Exodus 13:21-22.**

God used a fire to show the Israelites he was with them. You can use your campfire to help you remember that God is with you. Pray around your campfire.

Circle what you pray about.

someone who is sick

something you need

something to thank God for

something you liked about the Campfire Activity Award

your idea: _____

6 Help put out a fire. (do both)

☐ **Know the safe steps.**

Circle the right choice in each sentence.

1. Use {a stick/your foot} to spread out the coals.
2. Gently {dump/sprinkle} water over the coals.
3. {Stir/Pile up} the coals with a stick.
4. Sprinkle water again and stir again until everything is {dry/wet} and cold.
5. Carefully hold your {hot dog/hand} over the spot to be sure it is cold. But don't touch the spot.

☐ **Help an adult follow these steps.**

Answers to requirement 1:

1. BUILD
2. LED / A
3. ADS → S (ADULT down)
4. BUCKET
5. HAVE
6. CLOSE
7. BIGGER

Exploring ACTIVITY AWARD

To earn this award, do the things listed and check off each one:
- ☐ 1. Go on a nature hunt.
- ☐ 2. Walk outdoors.
- ☐ 3. Have fun outdoors.
- ☐ 4. Explore the sky.
- ☐ 5. See God's love.
- ☐ Extra Credit

Go on a nature hunt.

☐ **Find nature items.**
Here is a list of nature items to look for. See how many you can find.

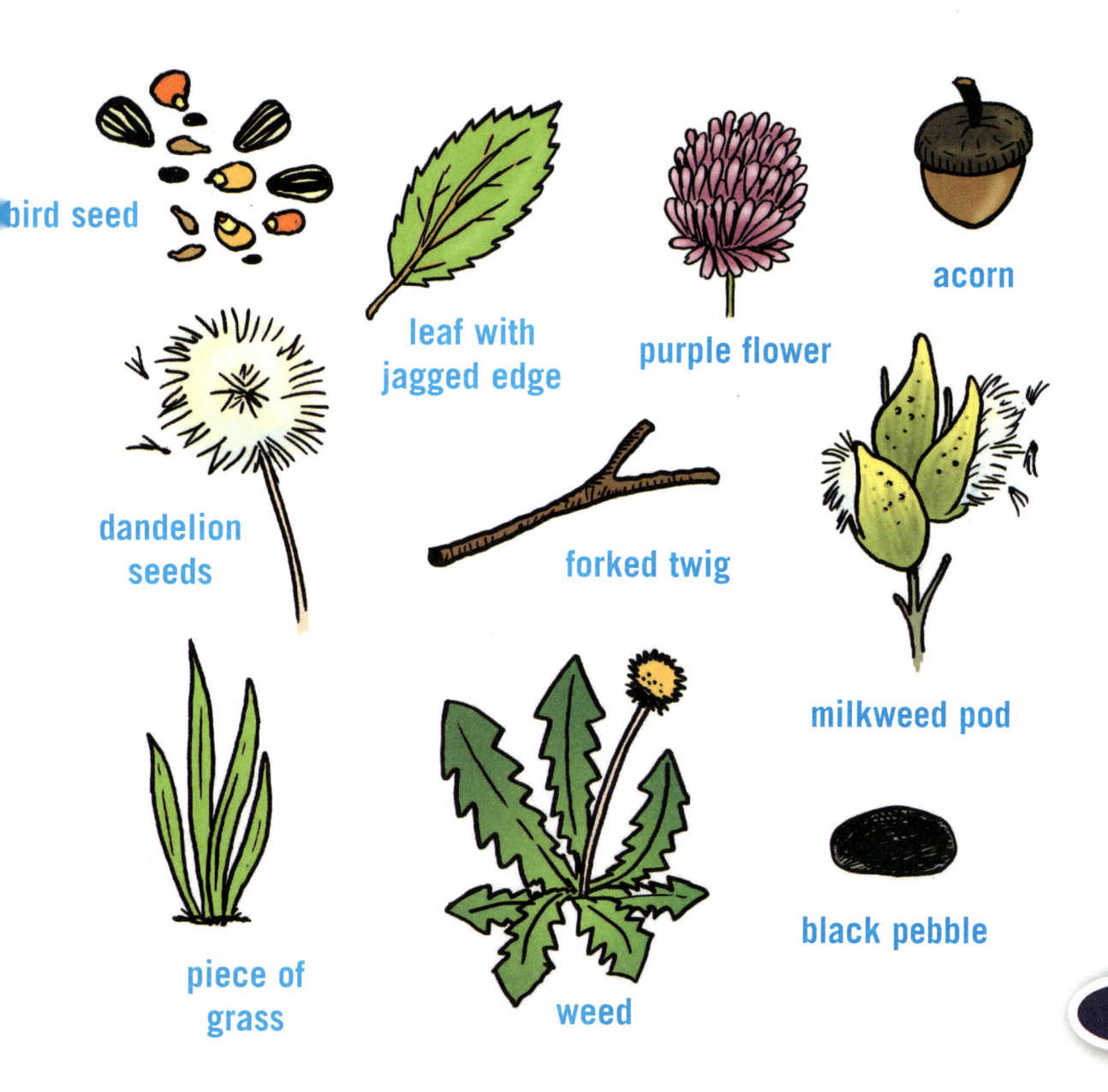

- bird seed
- leaf with jagged edge
- purple flower
- acorn
- dandelion seeds
- forked twig
- milkweed pod
- piece of grass
- weed
- black pebble

187

2 Walk outdoors. (do 1)

☐ **Hike**
Go on a hike. Discover nature along a trail. Or hike around your church or town. Draw something you see—plant, animal, or scene.

☐ **Photo Safari**
Go exploring with a camera. Take pictures of bugs, birds, trees, or whatever else you see. Show 1 of your pictures to your club.

☐ **Your Choice:** _____

3 Have fun outdoors. (do 1)

☐ **Explore at a park.**

How many kinds of animals or bugs do you see? _____

How many kinds of plants do you see? _____

☐ **Climb trees.**
Have an adult make sure the branches are safe.

☐ **Wade in a shallow stream.**
Be sure an adult is with you and watching. Circle what you can see under the water.

fish

mud

tadpoles

litter

plants

sand

pebbles

☐ **Your choice:** _____

4 Explore the sky.
(do 1)

☐ **Lie on your back and watch the clouds.**

What pictures can you see in the clouds? Use cotton balls here to show what some clouds look like.

☐ **Lie on your back and watch the stars.**

What can you see? The Milky Way? The Big Dipper? Use glitter here to show what some stars look like.

☐ **Watch a storm.**
Stay safe—stay indoors! Draw what it looked like. Tell someone what you saw.

☐ Your choice: _____

Exploring the Sky

by: _____

5 See God's love.

☐ **Memorize Psalm 108:4.**
What is greater than the huge greatness of the sky? Check 1.

☐ my strength   ☐ God's love   ☐ the trees

Extra Credit (do 1)

☐ Take part in a Pioneer Clubs Kids for Kids Hike. See www.pioneerclubs.org for information.

☐ Take a tour of some gardens or a nature area.

Fishing
ACTIVITY AWARD

To earn this award, do the things listed and check off each one:
- [ ] 1. Fishy Facts
- [ ] 2. Fishing Rules Game
- [ ] 3. Equipment
- [ ] 4. Go Fishing
- [ ] 5. Fish for People

1 Fishy Facts (do both)

[ ] **Where to Fish**

1. Fishing from solid ground is safest. Draw yourself fishing safely.
2. Fish like these places:
   rocky and weedy places
   logs and bridges
   deep water in summer
   shallow water when cool
   Draw fish where they might be in April.

[ ] **What to Bring**

Circle what you need to bring fishing. Cross out what you don't need.

bottle of water   pillow   first aid kit   hat   pajamas   sunscreen   stuffed animal
insect repellent   markers   snack   sunglasses

2 Fishing Rules Game (do all)

[ ] **Make a pole.**

Make a fishing pole by tying a string at least 3 feet (1 m) long to the end of a dowel rod. Tie a magnet to the other end of the string instead of a bobber and hook.

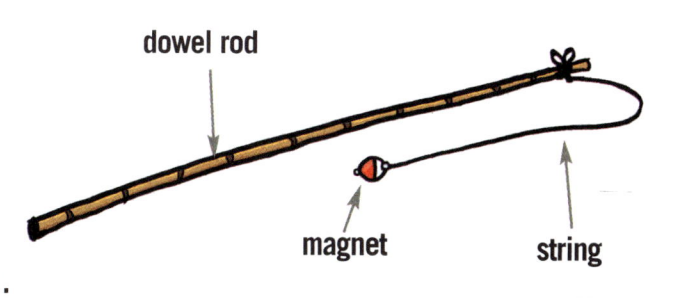

191

☐ **Make rule cards.**

Some of the sentences here are true fishing rules and some are bad ideas. Put each sentence on an index card. Put a paper clip on each index card. Lay the cards on the floor. This is your "pond."

☐ **Play your game.**

Take turns fishing for a rule card. When you catch 1, read it. (Other players may help.) Tell whether what the card says is a rule or a bad idea. Act out the correct action for what the card says.

3 Equipment

☐ **Learn about equipment.**

Have an adult help you find supplies for 1 type of fishing pole. Learn how to use it. Unscramble the names of the parts.

elni _____

koho _____

elpo _____

nirske _____

elre _____

ibta _____

brobeb _____

GOOD FISHING RULES:

- Fish with an adult.
- Wear a PFD (life jacket).
- Keep track of your hooks so no one sits on one.
- Fish from a safe place.
- Look around carefully before you cast.

BAD IDEAS:

- Complain about how the fish are biting.
- Break the fishing laws.
- Be noisy.
- Move quickly.
- Run around on shore.

Pole and Line — bobber, line, pole, sinker, hook, bait

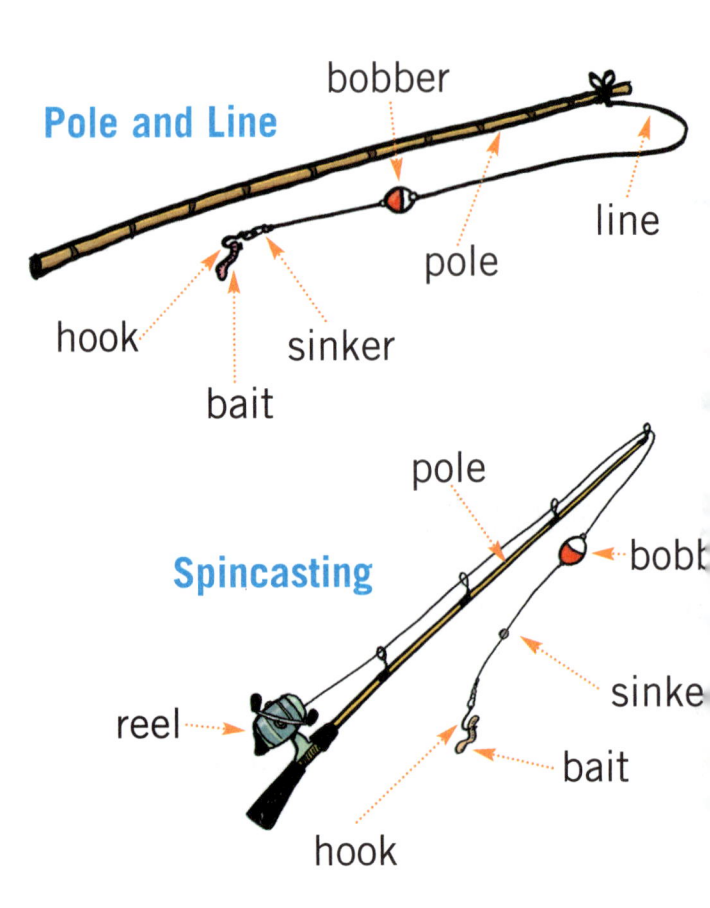

Spincasting — pole, bobber, sinker, bait, hook, reel

4 Go Fishing (do 1)

☐ **Fishing Practice**

Set up a fishing game. Cut out pictures of different kinds of fish. Clip a paper clip to each one. Spread out a sheet for a pond. Put the "fish" in the pond.

Use the pole from requirement 2. Show how to cast so your "hook" lands in the pond. When you catch a fish, show how to land it. What kind of fish did you catch? Draw it here.

Practice "Catch and Release"

Follow these steps for any fish you don't plan to eat. Ask an adult why they are important.

1. Carefully remove the hook.
2. Handle the fish as little as possible.
3. Gently put the fish back in the water.

☐ **Fishing Trip**

Take a trip to some water with an adult. Go fishing. Show an adult that you can:

___ Cast.

___ Land or reel in a fish. (Act it out if you don't catch anything.)

My Fish

5 Fish for People

☐ **Read or listen to Mark 1:17.**

Talk with an adult about what the verse means. Tell the adult 1 way you could fish for people.

193

Our Earth
ACTIVITY AWARD

To earn this award, do the things listed and check off each one:
- ☐ 1. Learn about natural resources.
- ☐ 2. Make a new item from an old one.
- ☐ 3. Care for the earth.
- ☐ 4. Look at God's earth.
- ☐ Extra Credit

1 Learn about natural resources. (do both)

☐ **What are natural resources?**

Natural resources are items in nature that can be used to make things or power things. Circle the pictures that show natural resources. Cross out the pictures that are not natural resources.

Answers at end of award.

☐ **Make a poster.**

Show ways people can take care of natural resources. *Ideas:*
- Turn off lights.
- Don't leave water running.
- Use recycle bins.
- Your ideas: _____

194

2 Make a new item from an old one. (do 1)

Learn to "reuse."

☐ **CD Ornament**

You will need:

- 2 old CDs
- cord, string, or yarn
- glue
- fake jewels, glitter, or other decorations
- scissors

Glue the 2 CDs together so the shiny sides face out. Tie some cord as shown to hang the ornament. Decorate with jewels, glitter, or other decorations.

☐ **Plastic Bag Holder**

You will need:

- old tube sock or knee sock
- twine
- scissors
- markers or fabric paint

Cut a hole about 1 inch (2.5 cm) wide in the toe of the sock. Stuff used plastic grocery bags in the top, 1 at a time. Tie the top of the sock closed with twine. Decorate with markers or fabric paint. Hang it from a hook or doorknob.

When your bag holder is empty, untie the top. Refill with plastic bags.

☐ **Your Choice:** _____

3 Care for the earth. (do 1)

☐ **Litter Bag**

You will need:

- paper lunch bags
- scissors
- glue
- markers
- old magazines or calendars

Decorate lunch bags with pictures from magazines or calendars. Or draw pictures. Write "Keep God's Earth Clean" on the bags. Put them in the car to use.

☐ **"Cleanup" Day**

Clean up litter from around your church, a walking trail, or park. Use gloves.

☐ Your Choice: _____

4 Look at God's earth.

(do both)

☐ **Read or listen to Genesis 1:31a.**

Circle what God said about the earth he made.

☐ **Play a game.**

Walk around outside and look at God's earth. Choose 1 item in nature that you really like. Tell players whether it's an *animal*, *vegetable*, or *mineral*. "Vegetable" means any plant. "Mineral" means made of stone or rock. Players try to discover what you chose. They ask questions that can be answered only "yes" or "no."

needs work

very good

Extra Credit

☐ Get permission and plant a tree or flowers. Have an adult help you. Make sure what you plant will get watered.

Answers to requirement 1:

sun and countryside, river, and trees

Outdoors
Activity Award

To earn this award, do the things listed and check off each one:
- ☐ 1. Outdoor Games
- ☐ 2. Outdoor Art
- ☐ 3. Green Thumb
- ☐ 4. Outdoor Life
- ☐ 5. Elijah's "Campout"
- ☐ Extra Credit

1 Outdoor Games (do 2)

☐ **Pass the Sponge**

Each team has a big sponge and 2 buckets. The first player on each team fills up the sponge from the first bucket. The player passes it backward over his or her head to the next player. The next player does the same thing, and so on to the end of the line. The last person squeezes the water into the empty bucket and passes the sponge back up the line. The first person fills and passes the sponge again. See how much water you have in your bucket after 3 (or 5) passes.

☐ **Spud**

Form a circle around IT. IT throws a ball into the air and calls a player's name. This player must run and get the ball and call, "Spud!" All other players run away during this same time. They must freeze when they hear "Spud!" The player with the ball may take 3 giant steps. Then he or she rolls the ball, trying to hit someone. If successful, the person who was hit is the new IT.

Devon!

☐ **Fill the Bottle**

Divide into teams. For each team, an adult lies on the ground. The adult holds an individual-size water bottle on his or her forehead. Teams line up opposite the adults. Each team has a small paper cup and a bucket of water. On "Go," the first player on each team dips a cup of water and runs to the adult. The player carefully pours the water into the adult's water bottle. Then he or she runs back to tag the next person.

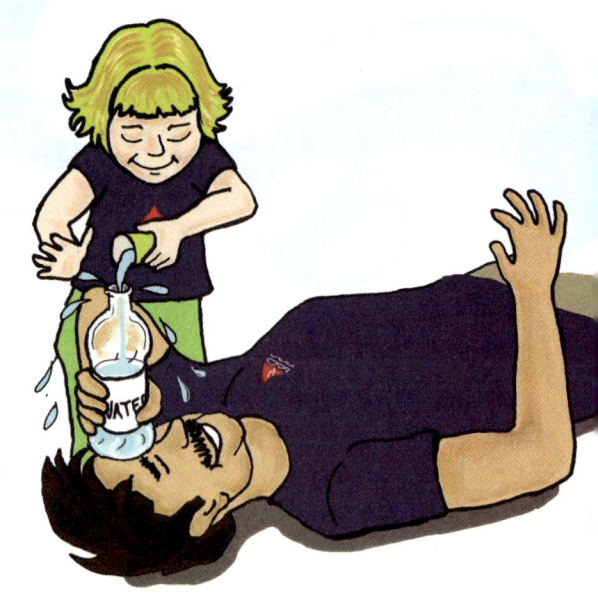

See which team can fill the water bottle the quickest. Watch out! The adult may get wet!

☐ **Hide and Seek**

☐ **Your Choice:** _____

2 Outdoor Art (do 1)

☐ **Splat Painting**

Lay a big sheet of paper on the ground. Roll a ball in paint. Throw it at the paper or roll it across. Try again with other colors. *Option:* Use pinecones instead of balls.

☐ **Sidewalk Chalk**

Get permission first. Draw on the sidewalk or parking lot with chalk. Make up cartoon strips. Or tell a story with pictures.

☐ **Your Choice:** _____

3 Green Thumb (do 1)

☐ **Plant flowers, vegetables, a tree, or herbs.**
Draw what the first leaves will look like here, or tape in the seed packet.

☐ **Tour a garden.**
In the frame above, draw what the garden looks like. Or draw some flowers, fruits, or vegetables you see.

☐ **Visit a farmer's market.**
Draw some fruits, vegetables, or flowers you see.

☐ **Pick flowers, vegetables, or herbs when they're ready.**
Get permission first.

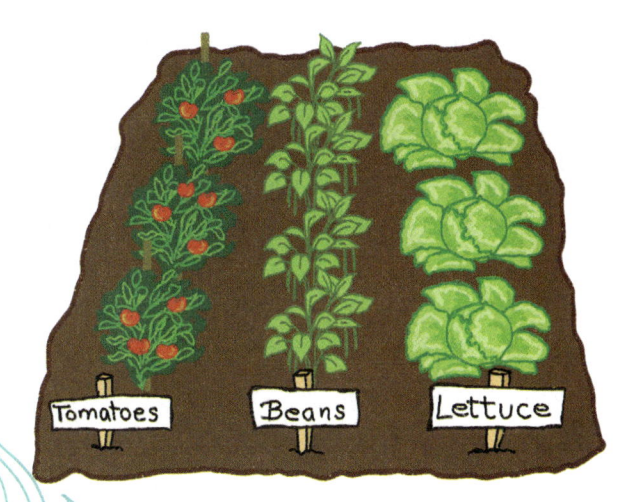

☐ **Water a garden or potted plants.**
Ask an adult how often the plants need water.

199

☐ **Weed a garden.**
Have an adult show you which plants are weeds.

☐ **Your choice:** _____

4 Outdoor Life (do 1)

☐ **Have a picnic.**

☐ **Have a barbecue.**

☐ **Set up a tent and pretend you're camping.**
Or hang blankets over a rope or picnic table.

☐ **Your choice:** _____

5 Elijah's "Campout"

☐ **Learn about Elijah.**
Read or listen to the story of Elijah's "campout" in 1 Kings 17:1-6. Elijah had a very special time with God in the out-of-doors. Pray to God, telling him 1 thing you like best about being in his out-of-doors.

Dear God, I really like _____.

Extra Credit (do 1)

☐ Camp out for real with your family, even if it's only in your backyard.

☐ Go on a Kids for Kids Hike with your club. See www.pioneerclubs.org for information.

Trees
ACTIVITY AWARD

To earn this award, do the things listed and check off each one:
- ☐ 1. Learn about trees.
- ☐ 2. Play with leaves.
- ☐ 3. Meet a tree.
- ☐ 4. Do an art project.
- ☐ 5. Read Genesis 1:11-12.
- ☐ Extra Credit

Learn about trees. (do both)

☐ **Know how trees help us.**
Circle what you like best about trees.

Trees give shade.

Trees give beauty.

Trees grow fruit and nuts.

Sap from some trees helps make these things.

Tree parts are used for medicine.

Trees give homes for animals.

Trees help clean the air.

Wood is used to make these things.

201

☐ **Enjoy food from a tree.**

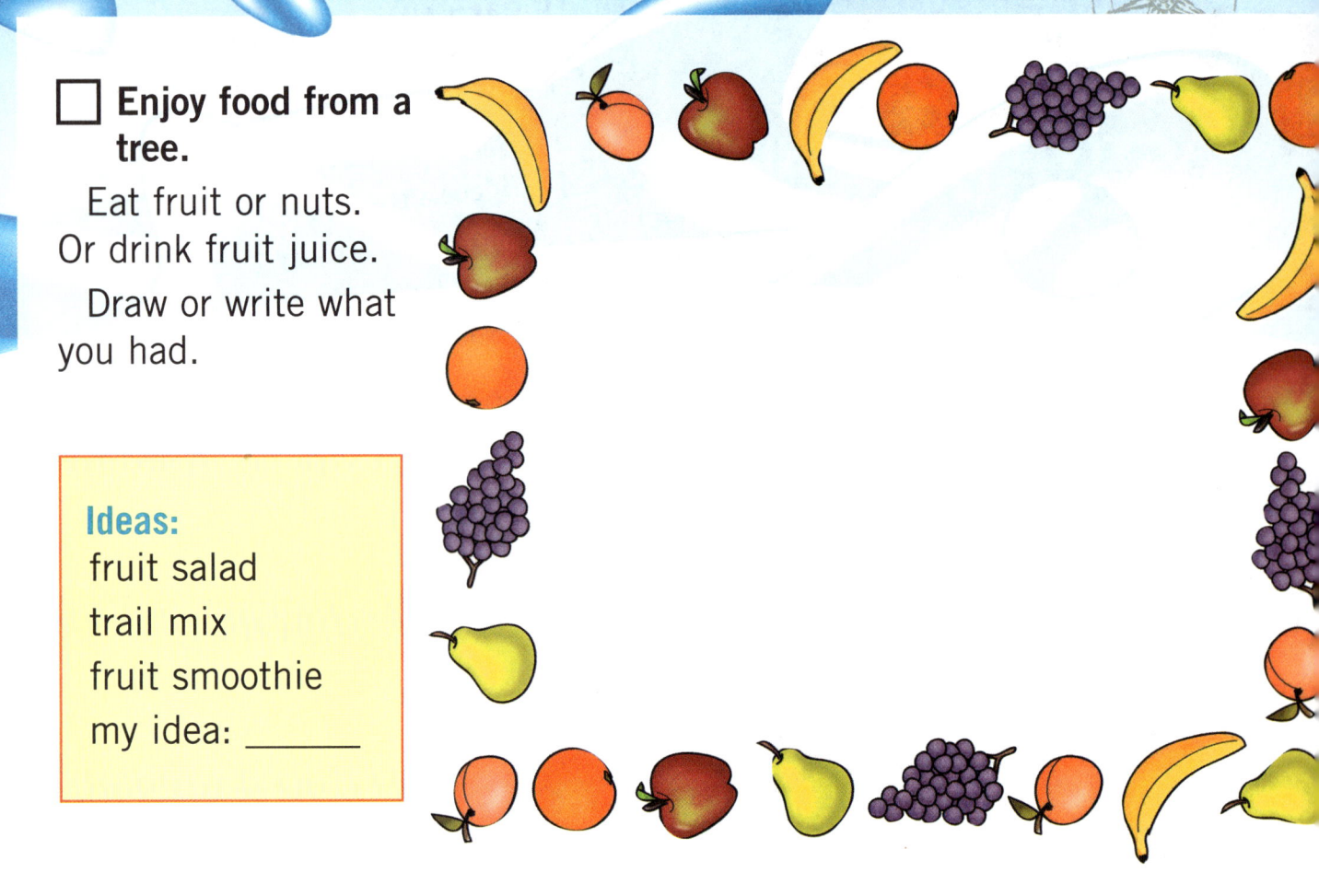

Eat fruit or nuts. Or drink fruit juice.

Draw or write what you had.

Ideas:
fruit salad
trail mix
fruit smoothie
my idea: _____

2 Play with leaves. (do 1)

☐ **Have a leaf-matching race.**

Put lots of different-shaped leaves in a pile. Two teams line up across from the pile. IT shows a leaf to the first 2 players and says, "Match it!" Players run to the pile. They find the same kind of leaf. Then they run back to their team. Then IT shows another leaf to the next 2 players. Keep doing this until all players have had a turn. IT picks the next IT from the team that finished first.

☐ **Have leaf-blowing contests.**

Find a partner. Each of you needs a leaf. Put your hands behind your back.
- See if you can blow your leaves so they land on top of each other.
- See who can blow his or her leaf across a finish line first.
- Put 1 leaf in the middle of a table. See who can blow it off the other person's side.

☐ Jump in a leaf pile.
☐ Rake leaves.
☐ Your choice: _____

3 Meet a tree. (do 2)

☐ **Go on a tree walk.**
With a grown-up, walk from tree to tree. Do something different at each tree. *Ideas:*

- Smell it.
- Crumple a leaf and smell it.
- Put your ear to the trunk and listen.
- Collect leaves.
- Touch the bark.
- Swing from a strong branch.
- Lie down and look up at the branch patterns.

How many trees did you visit? _____
How many different *kinds* of trees did you visit? _____
What did you see? Draw 1 or more of these.

Leaves   Bark
Fruit   Bird's nest
Acorns   Pinecones

☐ **Be a tree.**
With friends, act out how the parts of a tree work. Look at the picture to see how.

- *Trunk* supports branches.
- *Inner Bark* brings food to all parts of the tree.
- *Bark* protects the tree.
- *Roots* suck up water.

roots   bark   inner bark   trunk   inner bark   bark   roots

203

☐ **Choose a tree.**

Choose a favorite tree. Look closely at it. Use a magnifying glass. Look up into it and on the ground. Touch your tree, smell it, listen to it. See what animals or birds use it. Lie down, and pretend to be roots in the soil. How does that feel?

Draw a close-up of the part of your tree that you like best.

☐ Your choice: _____

4 Do an art project. (do 1)

☐ **Tree People**

You will need:
- tree parts
- paper
- glue

Collect objects that have fallen from a tree. Glue them to paper to make "tree people."

- leaf
- acorn
- seeds
- twig

☐ **Leaf Print**

You will need:
- white paper
- thin cardboard
- board
- plastic wrap
- mallet or hammer
- fresh leaves
- tape

Put thin cardboard on a flat board. Put white paper on the cardboard. Set a leaf on the white paper with the flat side down. Tape the stem in place. Cover the leaf with plastic wrap. Pound with a hammer, crushing the leaf. Pound all around the outer edges to get a good outline. The print on the paper is green from chlorophyll.

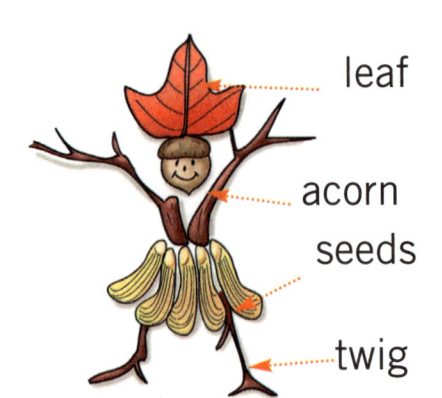

☐ **Leaf Suncatcher**

You will need:
- pressed leaves
- self-adhesive clear plastic
- scissors
- hole punch
- yarn or string

Peel the paper backing off the clear plastic. Arrange pressed leaves on the sticky side. Put another piece of plastic on top of them, sticky side down. Press together. Start in the center of the leaves and stroke out to push out bubbles. Cut around the leaves in a shape you like. Punch a hole in the top of the plastic. Put yarn through the hole. Hang this in a sunny window.

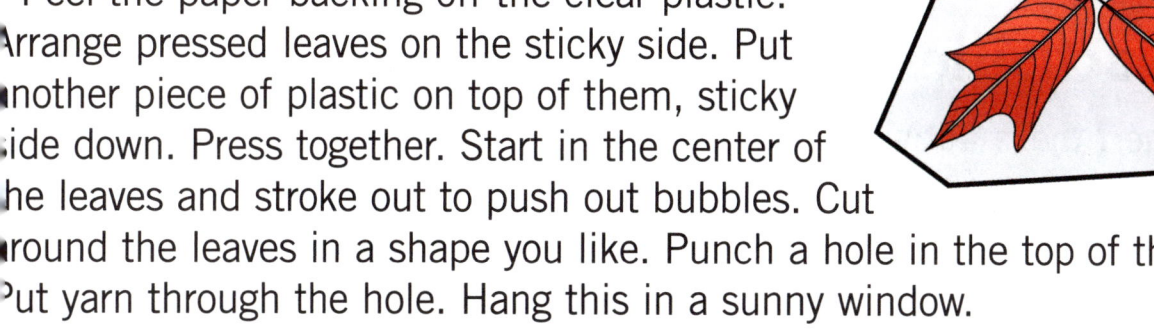

☐ Your Choice: _____

5 Read or listen to Genesis 1:11-12.

☐ **Learn about creation.**

How does God feel about the trees he made? Put a triangle around a face.
How do you feel about the trees he made? Put a square around a face.

Extra Credit (do 1)

☐ Plant a tree seed or sapling.
☐ Visit a garden center, nursery, or arboretum. Find out what trees need to be healthy.

Fitness Trail
ACTIVITY AWARD

To earn this award, do the things listed and check off each one:
- ☐ 1. Choose activities.
- ☐ 2. Set up your fitness trail.
- ☐ 3. Travel your fitness trail.
- ☐ 4. Whose body?
- ☐ Extra Credit

1 Choose activities.

☐ **Learn some fitness activities.**

Your fitness trail will have 7 stations. Try all the activities listed. Choose 1 for each station. Check off the 1 you choose.

Station 1—Keep Going

___ Walk fast for 4 minutes.

___ Jog in place for 3 minutes.

___ Skip for 2 minutes.

___ Your choice: _____

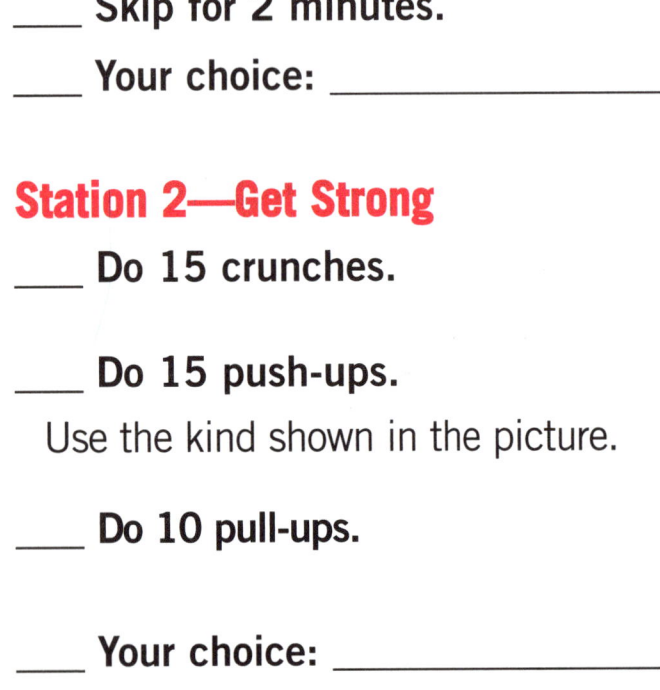

Station 2—Get Strong

___ Do 15 crunches.

___ Do 15 push-ups.

Use the kind shown in the picture.

___ Do 10 pull-ups.

___ Your choice: _____

crunches

push-ups

206

Station 3—Do Some Jumping

___ **Do 3 wall jumps.**

Squat down. Jump up and touch the wall as high up as you can.

___ **Do 10 star jumps.**

star jumps

___ **Your choice:** _____

Station 4—Use Your Arms

Use unopened soup cans as weights.

___ **Do 10 bicep curls.**

shoulder presses

___ **Do 10 shoulder presses.**

___ **Your choice:** _____

bicep curls

Station 5—Do More Jumping

___ **Leapfrog.**

Leapfrog over 6 small, sturdy stools set in a row.

___ **Jump over pillows.**

Jump over 6 pillows laid in a row.

___ **Your choice:** _____

Station 6—Balance

___ Walk along a 6-foot (2 m) board.

___ Balance on 1 foot for 30 seconds.

___ Your choice: _____

Station 7—Work Out with Balls

___ With a partner, toss and catch a ball 5 times.

___ Toss a ball against a wall and catch it 3 times.

___ Dribble a ball 5 times.

___ Your choice: _____

2 Set up your fitness trail.

☐ **Make a sign for each station.**

Write the name of the activity you chose. Or draw a picture of the activity.

3 Travel your fitness trail.

☐ **Go through the trail twice.**

Set up your trail with the signs. Jog or skip between stations. Try to do each station better the second time through. Fill in the chart on the next page.

	Day 1		Day 2	
	😀 good	😟 needs work	😀 good	😟 needs work
Station 1				
Station 2				
Station 3				
Station 4				
Station 5				
Station 6				
Station 7				

4 Whose body?

☐ Read or listen to 1 Corinthians 6:19-20.
Connect the start of the sentence to the right ending. Explain your choice.

I want to exercise   to show off.
   because my body belongs to God.
   to keep busy.

Extra Credit

☐ Find and use a real fitness trail. Have an adult with you to tell you which activities are safe for someone your age.

Games
ACTIVITY AWARD

To earn this award, do the things listed and check off each one:
- ☐ 1. Be a good sport.
- ☐ 2. Play guessing games.
- ☐ 3. Play tag games.
- ☐ 4. Play silly games.
- ☐ 5. Play old-time games.

1 Be a good sport.

☐ **Learn some good sport rules.**

Read 1 Timothy 4:12. Explain how each of these good sport rules fits with the verse.

- Take turns.
- Follow the rules.
- Be happy for the winner even when you don't win.
- Don't show off, just do your best.
- Be polite to the other players.

Make a poster with 1 or more of these rules that shows how kids can be good sports.

2 Play guessing games. (do 1)

☐ **Mittens**

Sit in a circle. All players put on mittens and close their eyes. IT gives 1 person an object. This gets passed around the circle so everyone can feel it. When the object comes back to the start, players guess what it was. IT says who guesses right. The first person to guess correctly is the next IT.

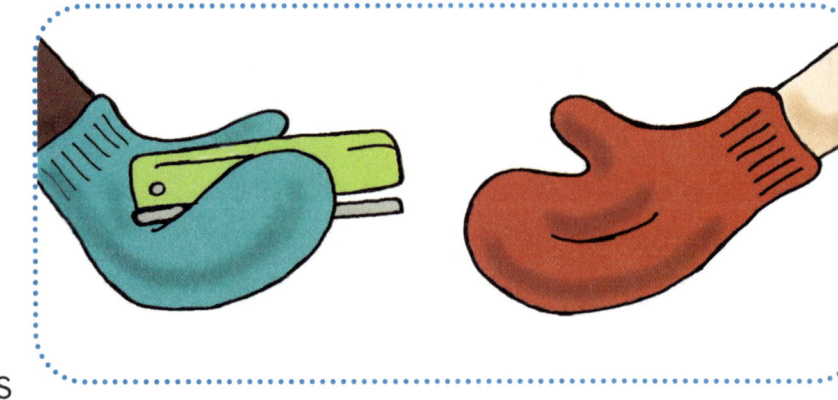

☐ **Roar**

Blindfold IT. Choose a player to stand in front of IT without IT knowing who. IT calls out an animal, such as "Lion!" The chosen player must make a lion noise so IT can guess who it is. If IT guesses right, the chosen player becomes IT. If IT guesses wrong, choose a new player. IT may call out a different animal each time. If IT guesses wrong 3 times, choose a new IT.

☐ **Number Pictures**

Everyone gets paper and markers. Each player writes a number from 1 through 10 on the paper. Then players draw pictures using these numbers. Guess the number each person started with.

Decide who made the most creative picture, the biggest picture, the smallest picture, the most colorful picture, and any other category you want.

☐ **Your Choice:** _____

3 Play tag games. (do 2)

☐ **Chasing a Cat**

Stand in a circle. The "dog" is in the middle. The rest are "cats." The dog begins saying, "Chasing a cat, chasing a cat, chasing a cat." When the dog says, "Chasing a cat NOW!" the cats run and the dog tries to catch someone. Whoever is caught is the new dog.

☐ **Skip and Hop Tag**

Play like regular tag. But IT calls out different ways to move, such as hopping, skipping, or walking like a duck.

"Chasing a cat NOW!"

211

☐ **Hoop Tag**

All players except 2—IT and a runner—stand in their own hula hoop. On "Go," IT starts chasing the runner. The runner may jump into any hula hoop. Then the player in that hoop becomes the new runner. If IT tags the runner, the tagged runner becomes IT.

☐ Your Choice: _____

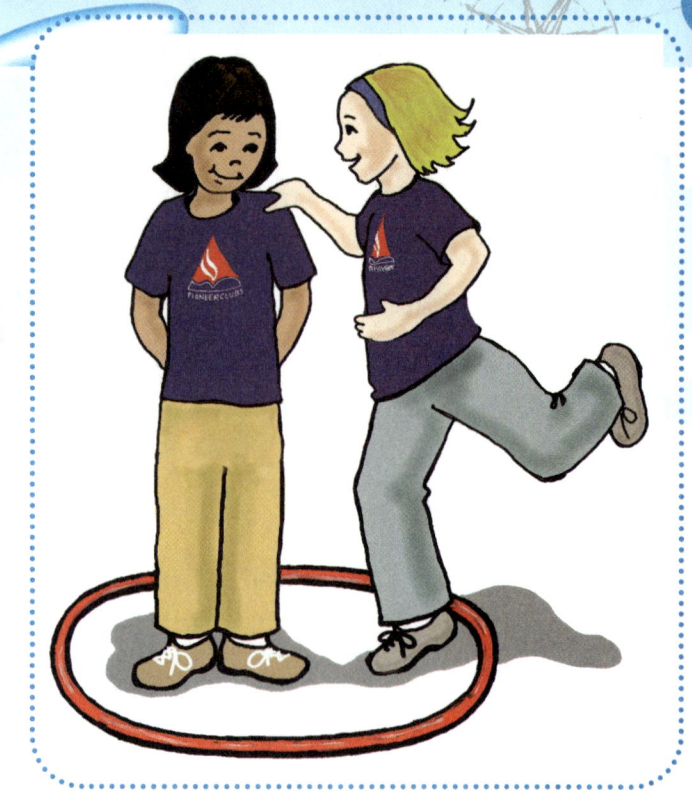

4 Play silly games. (do 2)

☐ **Make Me Laugh**

Form 2 teams. Teams line up facing each other. IT plays music. When the music stops, IT points to 1 team. IT counts to 10 while that team tries to make the other team laugh. They're not allowed to touch each other. The first person to laugh becomes IT. Make sure both teams get turns.

☐ **Statues**

Players run around while the music plays. They make funny movements and faces. When the music stops, they freeze. Anyone who moves is out.

☐ **Doggy, Doggy**

One player is the dog. The dog sits on a chair with eyes closed. Put a pencil (the "dog bone") behind the chair. Other players stand behind the dog. One sneaks up and steals the bone. Now all players put their hands behind their backs. They chant, "Doggy, doggy, where's your bone? Somebody stole it from your home!" The dog looks at the players. The dog gets 3 tries to guess who has the bone.

☐ Your Choice: _____

5 Play old-time games. (do 2)

☐ Marbles

☐ Jacks

☐ Cat's Cradle

☐ Hopscotch

☐ Leap Frog

☐ Your Choice: _____

213

Play Ball
ACTIVITY AWARD

To earn this award, do the things listed and check off each one:

☐ 1. Practice ball handling.
☐ 2. Play ball games.
☐ Extra Credit

1 Practice Ball Handling (do 6)

☐ **Bouncing**

Bounce a ball without catching it between bounces. See how many times you can bounce it in a row. When you get good at this, learn and use correct dribbling style. Or try it with your eyes closed.

☐ **Fake Egg Toss**

Every pair of players has a ball. Pretend the ball is a raw egg. Raw eggs go splat when they're dropped! Players face each other toe to toe. One tosses the ball to the other. If it's caught, that player takes 1 small step backward. Toss again. Move backward each time the ball is caught. When someone finally misses, he or she should say, "Splat!" and act out getting splatted by a raw egg.

☐ **Wall Bounce**

Throw a ball against a wall. Catch it after it bounces once on the ground. See how many times you can go without missing. Practice throwing the ball these ways:

> **2-handed**   **Right-handed**
> **Left-handed**   **Over your head**

Option: Try catching the ball without letting it bounce.

☐ **Partner Wall Bounce**

Play *Wall Bounce* with a partner. You throw the ball against the wall, and your partner catches it on 1 bounce. Then your partner throws it for you. Play until you have each caught the ball 10 times.

☐ **Bounce Pass**

Practice bounce-passing with a partner. Keep moving farther apart. Switch partners after a while.

☐ **Wall Kick**

Kick a ball gently against a wall. Let it come back to you and kick it again. See how many kicks you can do in a row.

☐ **Partner Wall Kick**

Play *Wall Kick* with a partner. Kick the ball gently against a wall. Your partner catches it and kicks it for you. Then you catch it and kick it. Do this 10 times. Now try kicking the ball back without catching it first.

☐ **Circle Catch**

Stand in a circle. The person with the ball calls someone's name and throws the ball to him or her. That person has to catch it. He or she calls someone else's name and throws the ball. See how long you can go without missing. As you get good at this, have everyone step back to make a bigger circle. Or try adding a second ball.

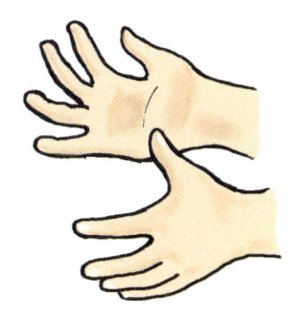

☐ **Kick Around**

IT is the music player. The other players stand in a circle, holding hands. Stretch the circle as big as it will go. Drop hands.

Have IT start some music. The players kick a ball from person to person. Don't kick the ball above waist high. Don't let the ball go out of the circle. When IT stops the music, stop kicking. The last person who kicked is the new IT.

2 Play Ball Games (do 4)

☐ **Kickball Mini Golf**

Use 9 empty boxes or wastebaskets for "mini golf holes." Put them on their sides. Play with a partner. Stand 10 feet (3 m) away from the first hole. Try to kick the ball into it. If you miss, your partner brings the ball back to you. You get 3 tries on each hole. Count how many holes you get the ball in.

☐ **Simon Says**

Each person needs a ball. Have some wastebaskets or boxes nearby for baskets. IT calls out actions to do with the ball. If IT says, "Simon says," players should do that action. If not, players should stay still. Sometimes IT will say how many times to do the action. Otherwise, players should keep going until a new action is called.

Examples:

Bounce!
Stop bouncing!
Toss! (Toss the ball in the air and catch it.)
Bounce once!
Roll to a partner!
Shoot! (Throw the ball into a basket.)

☐ **Ball Tag**

The player who is IT has a foam ball. IT tries to tag players by throwing the ball at them. Aim for legs only! If IT hits a player, that player becomes IT. If not, anyone may grab the ball and become IT.

☐ **5-Pin Soccer**

Find 5 2-liter plastic bottles. Put a little sand or water in each one. Screw the tops on. Line up the bottles in the middle of the playing area. Two teams line up on either side of the bottles. Players kick balls, trying to knock down pins. Players must stay behind their line. A referee sets pins back up and keeps score. See how many pins each team can knock down in 2 minutes.

☐ **Bounce-Pass Race**

Each team has a ball. Each team forms a line. Player 1 on each team bounce-passes the ball to Player 2. Player 2 bounce-passes the ball to Player 3, and so on. When the ball reaches the end of the line, send it back the way it came.

☐ **Basketball Free Throws**

Use a garbage can as the basket.

☐ **Kickball**

☐ **Soccer**

☐ **Your Choice:** _____

Extra Credit

☐ Play on a school or park district ball team.

Playing Together
ACTIVITY AWARD

To earn this award, do the things listed and check off each one:
- ☐ 1. Good Sports
- ☐ 2. Skill Games
- ☐ 3. Circle Games
- ☐ 4. Running Games
- ☐ 5. Ball and Balloon Games

1 Good Sports (do both)

☐ **Rules to Play By**

Put a Y for Yes by the rules that would keep your games fun and fair. Draw a line through the rules that would be unfair or no fun for some players.

_____ Take turns.   _____ Cheat if no one's looking.

_____ Keep the ball to yourself.   _____ Make fun of others.

_____ Be happy for the winners.   _____ Follow the game's rules.

☐ **Rule to Live By**

Read Matthew 7:12. Use the key to finish the sentence below:

A = ()   E = 👁   H = 🏠
M = ♠   O = ⊘   R = ☓
S = 🦟   T = ♥

God's rule for games and life is to treat _____ _____ _____ _____ _____ _____

as we would like _____ _____ _____ _____ to _____ _____ _____ _____ _____ us.

Explain to an adult how this rule and your good sport rules work together.

2 Skill Games (do 1)

☐ **How Do You Feel?**

The player who is IT goes out of the room. The other players choose a feeling, such as angry, scared, or shy. IT comes back to the room. IT points to a player and says, "How do you feel?" That player must act out the feeling. If IT can guess the feeling, the player becomes the new IT. If not, IT points to another player. IT may point to 3 players. If IT still can't guess, choose a new IT.

☐ **Switcheroo Simon Says**

Have 2 games of *Simon Says* going at the same time. Any player who misses just switches and joins the other game.

☐ **Ankle Jump Rope**

Play with 3 players and a rope at least 9 feet (3 m) long. Tie the ends of the rope to make a large loop. Have 2 players put the rope around their ankles. They move apart until the rope is tight and off the ground.

A third player, the jumper, jumps inside the rope with both feet. When the jumper jumps out again, both feet may be outside on the same side of the ropes. Or one foot may be outside on each side. The jumper jumps back inside and then out again. Make up a pattern of which side the jumper should land on. When the jumper lands *on* the rope, change jumpers.

3 Circle Games (do 2)

☐ **Zoom**

Form a circle. Everyone pretends to drive a race car. The first person turns to a player on one side and says, "Zoom!" This person turns to next player and says, "Zoom!"

At any time, a player may say, "Errt!" That means the race car "turns"—so the zooms go the other way around the circle. See how fast you can pass the zooms.

☐ **Drop the Handkerchief**

Play like *Duck-Duck-Goose.* When IT drops a handkerchief behind one of the other players, that person must pick it up before running to tag IT.

☐ **Favorites**

Sit in a circle. IT calls out "Food!" and rolls a ball to someone. This player names a favorite food and rolls the ball to someone else.

At any time, IT may call out another kind of favorite to name, such as *toys, books, games, school subjects, animals.* Players may not name anything that someone else has named.

After 3 or 4 switches, choose a new IT.

☐ **What I Like**

The first player acts out something he or she likes, such as jumping rope. The others in the circle guess what the player likes. Then it's the next person's turn.

☐ **Your Choice:** _____

4 Running Games (do 2)

☐ **2-Headed Monster**

To make IT, 2 players hold hands. The other players stand in a circle around IT. Players run when IT calls out, "Here comes the 2-headed monster!" When IT catches someone, that player joins hands with IT. Now IT calls out, "Here comes the 3-headed monster!" Continue adding people—and heads on the monster—until all players are caught.

☐ **Sack Race**

Every racer needs a large sack. Racers step into the sack and hold it up. At "Go!" everyone hops toward the finish line. *Option:* Very large rubber bands like those used for exercising can be used to hold each racer's ankles close together.

☐ **Kick the Can**
☐ **Your Choice:** _____

5 Ball and Balloon Games (do 2)

☐ **Crazy Balls**

IT starts 2 large balls rolling in the playing area. Players use their feet to keep the balls moving. Don't let a ball stop! Every minute, IT adds another ball. See how many you can keep moving at the same time.

☐ **Balloon Bump**

Players stand in a circle, holding hands. Have one person toss up a balloon. Players move around to keep the balloon in the air. They may hit it any way they like as long as they don't let go of each others' hands.

How long can you and your friends keep a balloon in the air? Have someone time you.

☐ **1-2-3!**

Players stand in a circle and count together: "1-2-3!" On 3, a player throws a foam ball (or bean bag) high into the air. Another player must catch it before it hits the ground. If someone does, 2 players toss balls the next time. Each time all balls are caught, add another ball. If a ball is missed, take away a ball.

☐ **Your Choice:** _____

Relays
ACTIVITY AWARD

To earn this award, do the things listed and check off each one:
- ☐ 1. Skill Relays
- ☐ 2. Relays with Props

1 Skill Relays (do 4)

☐ **Chimp Relay**

Players must move with feet apart, holding their ankles.

☐ **Keep It Neat**

You will need 1 shirt and 1 clothes hanger for each player. Put shirts and hangers in a big pile. Tie a rope across the room for a clothesline.

Players run to the pile. They find 1 clothes hanger and hang 1 shirt on it. They hang this on the clothesline. Then they run back to tag the next player.

☐ **Knotty Relay**

Have a rope for each team. Tie a loose knot in the rope for each player.

The first player on each team unties 1 knot and passes the rope to the next player, and so on.

If everyone knows how to tie knots, race again. Have each person tie a knot and pass the rope along.

☐ **Snowshoe Relay**

Every player gets a pair of "snowshoes" (2 sheets of newspaper). Players shuffle on their snowshoes to the finish line and run back to tag the next player. If a snowshoe rips, they must run to the "store" (IT) for a new one. Then they must start again where they left off.

☐ **Sock Hop**

Each player takes off 1 shoe. Make a big pile of all the shoes. Teams line up an equal distance from the pile. Players hop on 1 foot to the pile and find their shoe. They put it on and run back to tag the next player.

☐ **Roller Relay**

Mark a finish line not too far away from the start line. Players lie down and roll to the finish line.

2 Relays with Props (do 4)

☐ **Noodle Relay**

Players run while holding a swim noodle between their knees.

☐ **Pingpong Pickup**

Put a pingpong ball for each team member in a hula hoop. Put a big container in the center of the hula hoop. Team members take off shoes and socks. They sit around the hula hoop. On "Go," the first player uses toes to pick up a ball and put it in the container. Then the next player goes, and so on.

☐ **Jump Rope Relay**

Each player runs to a jump rope and jumps 3 times. Then the player runs back to tag the next player.

☐ **Ball of String**

Each team passes a ball of string or yarn down the line. Each person must keep hold of the string so that the ball is unwinding. Then players pass the ball back. They wind the string back up as they go.

☐ **Sponge Relay**

Play on a warm day—outdoors! Each team lines up by a bucket. Each bucket has the same amount of water in it. An empty bucket is by each team's finish line. Players soak up water with a big sponge. They carry the sponge to the empty bucket and squeeze the water in. See whose bucket has the most water after all players have taken a turn. Or play until 1 team's bucket is full.

☐ **Beanbag Feet**

Players carry a beanbag on 1 foot. If 1 falls off, that player must stop and put it back on.

☐ **Your Choice:** _____